Deep-Dive Terraform on Azure

Automated Delivery and Deployment of Azure Solutions

Ritesh Modi

apress®

Deep-Dive Terraform on Azure: Automated Delivery and Deployment of Azure Solutions

Ritesh Modi
Hyderabad, Telangana, India

ISBN-13 (pbk): 978-1-4842-7327-2 ISBN-13 (electronic): 978-1-4842-7328-9
https://doi.org/10.1007/978-1-4842-7328-9

Managing Director, Apress Media LLC: Welmoed Spahr
Acquisitions Editor: Smriti Srivastava
Development Editor: Laura Berendson
Coordinating Editor: Shrikant Vishwakarma

Cover designed by eStudioCalamar

Cover image designed by Pexels

Distributed to the book trade worldwide by Springer Science+Business Media LLC, 1 New York Plaza, Suite 4600, New York, NY 10004. Phone 1-800-SPRINGER, fax (201) 348-4505, e-mail orders-ny@springer-sbm. com, or visit www.springeronline.com. Apress Media, LLC is a California LLC and the sole member (owner) is Springer Science + Business Media Finance Inc (SSBM Finance Inc). SSBM Finance Inc is a **Delaware** corporation.

For information on translations, please e-mail booktranslations@springernature.com; for reprint, paperback, or audio rights, please e-mail bookpermissions@springernature.com, or visit www.apress.com/rights-permissions.

Apress titles may be purchased in bulk for academic, corporate, or promotional use. eBook versions and licenses are also available for most titles. For more information, reference our Print and eBook Bulk Sales web page at www.apress.com/bulk-sales.

Any source code or other supplementary material referenced by the author in this book is available to readers on GitHub via the book's product page, located at www.apress.com/978-1-4842-7327-2. For more detailed information, please visit www.apress.com/source-code.

Printed on acid-free paper

While writing this book, I grew into a person who has more patience, perseverance, and tenacity. I would like to dedicate the book to the people who mean the world to me. I am talking about my mother, Bimla Modi; my wife, Sangeeta; and my daughter, Avni.

Table of Contents

About the Author

Ritesh Modi works for Microsoft as a senior engineer. He has served as a Microsoft regional director as well as a regional lead for Microsoft certified trainers in past.

Ritesh is an architect, senior evangelist, cloud architect, published author, speaker, and known leader for his contributions in the areas of blockchain, Ethereum, datacenter, Azure, bots, cognitive services, DevOps, artificial intelligence, and automation. He has more than a decade of experience in building and deploying enterprise solutions for customers. He has contributed multiple times to the open source AzureRM provider.

About the Technical Reviewer

Nicky Saini is a passionate technology enthusiast with 13+ years of valuable experience in the IT industry. He currently works with UBS as a cloud SRE. He has completed a number of certifications in the cloud and container worlds. He has worked with different tools and technology and has hands-on experience in DevOps methodologies on the cloud platform, deploying and provisioning secure and robust cloud platforms with automation tools. He is a self-learner and likes to explore new tools and technology.

Acknowledgments

Writing this book has been a fantastic experience. I owe a lot to the people who motivated me with their encouragement. I would like to thank so many people for making this book happen.

Thank you to the people who inspire me to push myself and who ultimately make everything worthwhile, the three wonderful ladies in my life: my mother, Bimla Modi; wife, Sangeeta Modi; and daughter, Avni Modi.

Thanks, of course, to the Apress team. I would like to thank my editors for providing direction at each stage of the publishing process and guiding me through it. I would also like to thank my technical reviewer who read the book multiple times and gave incredibly useful feedback. Finally, I thank everyone who has helped me learn both Azure and Terraform through numerous discussions and projects. This book wouldn't have been possible without each one of them.

Introduction

Azure has matured as a cloud provider over a period of time. It provides numerous capabilities and helps organizations focus on their core business aspects while automating tasks based on standardization, consistency, and uniformity. Building and managing infrastructure is an important activity on Azure, and Terraform is one of the leading infrastructure-as-code (IaC) frameworks to effectively do so. It is one of the leading IaC platforms for managing a large variety of target environments. Terraform helps in managing the entire lifecycle of the infrastructure, from provisioning to teardown. Terraform and Azure providers are well maintained, are updated on a weekly basis with new resources and bug fixes, and have acceptance from a large community of developers.

Organizations need confidence and a high level of predictability when deploying on Azure. They want to implement changes to environments in a consistent manner, and Terraform helps achieve this using its idempotent deployments and configuration-based language. Terraform provides numerous concepts and artifacts that are used during both development and deployment. It internally manages idempotent deployments using a state file. Its scripting language is quite versatile and helps developers write easy to complex configurations. It is extensible and allows developers to add newer resources and author modular configurations that are generic and reusable across multiple deployments, environments, and solutions.

Bringing Terraform and Azure together is a win-win proposition for organizations and developers. It helps in easily automating the environment provisioning while ensuring that the process is quick, reliable, and cost-effective. This book is an attempt to educate readers about possible approaches for using Terraform alongside Azure. Each chapter builds on the prior chapter and slowly and steadily takes the reader through all the major concepts of Terraform in the context of Azure. After reading this book, readers who are new to Terraform will be able to start writing Terraform configurations, and experienced developers will be able to apply the Terraform best practices and write complex configurations.

INTRODUCTION

This book is meant for both developers and architects to effectively implement and deploy environments using Terraform on Azure.

I hope readers will find this journey fruitful in their quest for learning and employ their newfound knowledge in their solutions and projects.

Happy learning!

CHAPTER 1

Infrastructure as Code

Before the advent of cloud computing, most infrastructure environments were built manually. Building all the environments including the production environment was done by infrastructure engineers using manual techniques and processes. There was some scripting and automation, but even those scripts were executed manually. The infrastructure would generally not undergo changes and would be exclusively created and maintained by infrastructure engineers. There was not much need to scale the infrastructure, neither were there disruptive changes to it apart from failing hardware. This manual maintenance would work fine in most cases.

Things have changed rapidly over the years, especially after the cloud gained significant traction with more and more organizations moving their applications and deployments to the cloud. The cloud brings agility and flexibility to both provisioning and maintaining applications. This agility is in terms of faster, frequent, consistent and more predictable deployments.

The application architecture and deployment models have also changed during the last few years. Monolith applications are getting broken into smaller microservices, with each having their own development and deployment lifecycle, and each having their own infrastructure requirements in terms of size, performance, scalability, disaster recovery, and availability.

With this increase in size, complexity, and number of infrastructure deployments, it was becoming increasingly difficult to continue with the traditional manual ways to administer, manage, and configure infrastructure. Moreover, the manual steps to create the infrastructure environment led to delays due to lower consistency, predictability, and standardization.

© Ritesh Modi 2021
R. Modi, *Deep-Dive Terraform on Azure*, https://doi.org/10.1007/978-1-4842-7328-9_1

There was a need for automation to provision, manage, and evolve infrastructure with higher consistency. In addition, there was a need to be more predictable in deployments to gain a higher level of confidence and a need for standardization such that provisioning become process dependent rather than human dependent.

It also started becoming evident during this time that infrastructure is a shared responsibility among developers and operations similar to an application, rather than being owned by a handful of infrastructure engineers.

A new paradigm called *infrastructure as code* (IaC) emerged because of all the challenges faced with manual infrastructure deployment and configuration. IaC helps by treating infrastructure as part of the overall solution by converting it into code and taking it through the same lifecycle, steps, and process that an application would undergo. It ensures that infrastructure becomes part of the software engineering practices similar to an application and that all the engineering principles and processes are applied to it. This includes authoring of infrastructure code, version control, different levels and types of testing (unit, integration, acceptance), linting, and more.

Terraform is a tool that helps in managing resources, both on-premises as well as on the cloud, and is based on the concept of IaC. Before we understand Terraform, it is important to understand the concept of IaC.

Introduction to IaC

IaC is a process of converting infrastructure to code. It is about treating code reflecting infrastructure similar to application code and having it undergo the same engineering practices and principles as the application code. This means version controlling the infrastructure code; collaborating with other developers on it; validating it by running of tests (unit, integration, and acceptance tests); performing code linting, code reviews, and other quality checks; creating documentation; and deploying it to multiple environments.

However, authoring IaC and adopting engineering practices is just one aspect of IaC. Another important facet of IaC is how we convert the infrastructure into code. A simple strategy is to write bash or PowerShell scripts and execute them periodically or on-demand, passing in different configuration data as parameters to provision, de-provisioning, manage and administer the environments.

This approach is an acceptable way to work with an environment, and is known as the *imperative* way of managing an environment. In the imperative way, the author must provide instructions about how to manage an environment. It must explicitly provide instructions about provisioning, deleting, or updating an environment and also has to provide configuration data associated with each environment.

IaC does not mandate but prefers the declarative paradigm for managing the environment. *Declarative* IaC deals with "what" should be managed instead of "how." Under the declarative way, the author provides the configuration of the environment and its associated resources. The author does not provide instructions about whether resources should be created, deleted, or updated with the given configuration. It is the responsibility of the automation and tools used for IaC to determine within the current context whether it will provision, delete, or update the resources in the environment.

Resources have their lifecycle: they are provisioned, updated, and deleted. While undergoing this lifecycle, they should be actively administered and governed. *Administration* refers to activities related to patching, availability, and performance of the resource. *Governance* relates to ensuring resource compliance with organizational policies and standards, and *optimization* refers to monitoring resource, identifying cost reduction opportunities, and improving performance.

Figure 1-1 shows the lifecycle of a resource in an IT development environment. A resource is provisioned, undergoes through updates, and is eventually deleted after a period of time. During this time, it should be managed, administered, monitored, and governed.

Figure 1-1. *Resource lifecycle within an IT development environment*

Declarative IaC helps in defining the configuration of the resource once and ensures that it can be used for provisioning, updating, and deleting the resource.

The configuration defined for the resource is the desired state of the resource, and all resources represents the desired state of the environment. The tool used for implementing IaC will evaluate the configuration code with the actual deployed resource configuration to determine whether it should provision, update, or delete the resource.

If the configuration in code is the same as the actual deployed configuration, then no changes are applied; however, any deviation from the current state to the desired state in the environment would lead to the creation, deletion, or updating of the resource.

Figure 1-2 shows that the configuration determines "what" to manage, while the comparison with actual environment helps in determining the intent (should the resource be updated, deleted, or created. New resources would be provisioned if they are not already present in the actual environment, updated if they already exist but differ in configuration, and deleted if the resource exists in the target environment but not in the configuration (a delete in Terraform needs an `explicitly` executed).

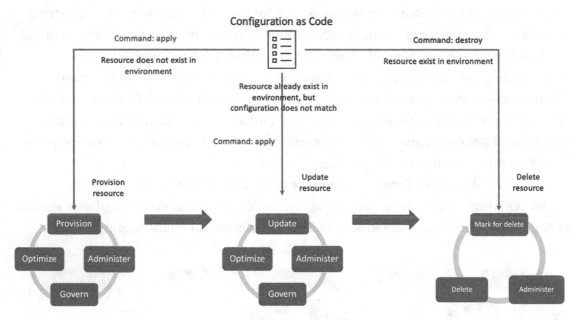

Figure 1-2. *Configuration as code determines "what" to manage, while the current context determines the intent*

The apply command in this context means to apply the configuration available in code to the target environment. It could mean provisioning or updating resources. It would provision the resource if it does not already exist, update the resource if any of its configuration have deviations between the existing and desired state. The command `destroy` would delete the resources.

The process and steps to administer, govern, and optimize resources could be done using the imperative way of managing resources.

It is quite evident that there should be specialized tools available to implement IaC. There are many tools like Terraform, Ansible, Chef, Desired State Configuration (PowerShell DSC), Salt, Puppet, and Pulumi. Each tool has its own way of implementing IaC; however, the end result is almost always the same: managing the infrastructure environment using code.

This book focuses on Terraform as the IaC tool and also uses Azure as its target cloud platform.

Benefits of IaC

The processes of environment provisioning and deployments have undergone significant changes over the years and have been further accentuated with the emergence of cloud computing. IaC provides benefits when used as part of a long-term strategy. The following sections explain some of the benefits of adopting IaC.

Faster Release Cycles and High-Quality Delivery

With IaC in place, the infrastructure components are created using verified code without human intervention. This leads to consistent and predictable deployments, reducing human error and time spent in fixing those errors. Better rollback ability is available by default due to version-controlled versions of code. Eventually the software delivery is faster and quicker to production due to better predictability.

Process Dependency, Standardization, and Consistency

Removing manual deployments, executing scripts, and using tools like Terraform help in bringing upon higher reliance on process rather than individual skill and availability. Both the code and the infrastructure it manages can be standardized to bring better manageability and thereby reduce the overall cost of ownership of resources. Both developers as well as operations have the same view of the infrastructure. Multiple environments without differences between them can be created with ease, which brings in a higher level of consistency in infrastructure provisioning.

Predictability and Idempotency

The environments provisioned should not change unless there is a change in the infrastructure code itself. Rerunning the same configuration multiple times with the same values should not change the resource configurations. The whole idea behind predictability and idempotency is that, given a set of inputs, the outputs will always remain the same. If the output can change for the same input, it is not predictable and idempotent. IaC ensures that authored configurations are both predictable and idempotent.

Agility and State of Readiness

Adopting IaC ensures that the code that provisions the infrastructure is quality controlled and verified. This code can be used at any time to provision the new environment as well as to bring about changes to the existing environment. This is the state of readiness with regard to software infrastructure. Maintaining such a state of readiness eventually results in higher agility to do more deployments and releases more frequently.

Better Collaboration Between Dev and Operations

Authoring an IaC configuration is a joint responsibility of both developers and operations. While the initial configuration is authored by developers, it is eventually used by operations to update and manage the resources. Having joint responsibility improves the coordination and results in better collaboration between multiple teams.

Compliance to Organization Policies

It is possible to lay down policies that should be adhered to while provisioning new or updating existing resources. Examples include resources that should be provisioned in select regions only, resources that should be a specific size, and so on.

Enables Effective DevOps

With developers and operations having joint responsibility for the infrastructure environment and having the infrastructure-related code go through the same engineering process as an application, the DevOps continuous integration pipelines are being used for code reviews, linting, and testing. Similarly, continuous delivery and deployment pipelines are used for validating the code by deploying it early in a sandbox environment. This practices ensures that both the application and the infrastructure code are validated and verified before deployment to production, which ensures that the quality of deployment and release is superior compared to the manual approach of deployment.

Terraform as a Means to IaC

Hashicorp's Terraform is one of the leading open source, cross-platform, multicloud, hybrid IaC tools available to provision and manage IT and development resources on both on-premises and any cloud. It was built using the Golang language and also provides its own scripting language known as the Hashicorp Configuration Language (HCL). HCL is a declarative language that helps developers write "what" should be provisioned as part of the infrastructure. You will start using Terraform in Chapter 2.

Terraform provides all the features and components needed to implement IaC within an engagement. As mentioned before, it provides a declarative language for defining the configuration of resources. The resources configured by Terraform are managed by Terraform with the help of state file which is an advance topic describe in details in subsequent chapters.

Terraform provides a CLI based executable with the help of which all Terraform commands can be executed. It is one of the important part of Terraform and all interactions with Terraform happen using this CLI.

The CLI helps in executing commands, and those commands are then executed against the actual target environment based on configurations defined within the scripts.

The commands can be executed manually or can be executed as a series of steps from orchestration tools like Jenkins and Azure DevOps.

All the necessary commands (the details of which we will go into in the next two chapters) to enable IaC—such as planning a configuration deployment, applying (provisioning and updating) and deleting resources from actual target environment and managing configurations are available with Terraform.

Terraform provides detailed logs and auditing features and is capable of being used in a multiteam environment. It provides a locking feature that allows a queued execution of Terraform script within a multi-team environment. The scripts can be version controlled, and it can be tested using the Golang testing facilities (something we will go deeper into in Chapter 8).

Every HCL configuration has two main elements: the configuration script and the configuration values. The script is generally considered static and does not change from one environment to another, whereas the configuration values are environment specific. Terraform helps in separating the script from configuration values and this enables provisioning multiple similar environments that only differ in configuration values. This feature helps developers write generic Terraform scripts that can be used in deployment pipelines to provision multiple environments each with unique configuration values.

Terraform configurations are idempotent in nature. It means that for a given configuration values, the script will always generate the same output and resource configuration irrespective of the number of times they are executed.

Summary

This was the first chapter of the book. In this introductory chapter, we went a bit back in history to explore the manual way of executing deployments and the challenges involved using them. You learned that the cloud is changing the way deployments are planned and defined and how modern infrastructure need more predictability, consistency, and agility to bring faster releases. The IaC paradigm was introduced in this chapter. We understood that IaC helps in mitigating almost all the challenges inherent in manual infrastructure deployments, and we also learned about the benefits of IaC. The chapter also introduced Terraform as one of the most popular IaC platform. Terraform provides all the important features of IaC and is an enterprise-ready tool for managing infrastructure.

In the next chapter, you will understand the Terraform architecture, explore its workflow, and also get a high-level overview by writing and executing our first Terraform configuration.

CHAPTER 2

Azure and Terraform

In this chapter, we'll introduce Terraform at a higher level by creating a simple configuration, we'll follow the process of executing the configuration against Azure, and we'll understand the actions performed during this time before getting into the depths of Terraform concepts and configuration. This will not only make the following chapters easy to follow but also help readers understand the big picture of writing and executing Terraform scripts.

The focus of this chapter will be on understanding the architecture of Terraform, setting up the development environment, setting up an Azure subscription, writing our first Terraform configuration, and understanding the Terraform workflow.

Terraform Architecture

Technically, Terraform is a tool to orchestrate consumption of remote APIs (services) exposed by a provider. For example, each cloud platform provides multiple APIs for managing its resources. These APIs can be invoked using client-side libraries written in any programming language for which an SDK exists. Terraform provides a platform to create such providers easily for the management of resources by consuming their APIs. These APIs can also be called *upstream* APIs.

As mentioned before, Terraform is written in Golang and it is quite easy for it to consumes API's directly using request-response objects. This practice is acceptable however, a better approach is to write a library that encapsulates the low-level HTTP request-response communication and exposes a well-defined client that can be used by anyone to talk to the upstream APIs. This client library will then become a provider library to consume its remote upstream APIs. Each cloud platform typically provides a client library for its APIs. The client library is responsible for connecting and invoking remote API endpoints specific to that provider.

© Ritesh Modi 2021
R. Modi, *Deep-Dive Terraform on Azure*, https://doi.org/10.1007/978-1-4842-7328-9_2

The client libraries are not used by the Terraform core directly. Terraform has a concept of plugins, and it decouples the implementation of plugins from the core. Terraform can interact with multiple plugins at the same time using remote procedure calls. In computing parlance, a *plugin* is a reusable module or software that can be "plugged in." Plugins are based on the extensible architectural principle, which means that either it can be plugged in as a new component or can replace an existing component such that the application continues to run without recompilation and redeployment. The new component can be plugged in at runtime without any downtime and disruption. Terraform is based on extensible architecture and uses a plugin model. Terraform supports two types of plugins.

- Providers

- Provisioners

We will look at providers in this chapter and provisioners will be covered in subsequent chapters.

The Terraform core comprises the important component implementation like Terraform command-line interface, its commands, state management, backend, and workspace management. The core itself does not contain any cloud resources; resources that we are interested in provisioning and managing for our solutions. Terraform provides a provider SDK that can be used to implement cloud providers. The Terraform core can communicate with any provider as long as the provider adheres to and implements the Terraform provided types and contracts in the provider SDK. All the cloud platforms including Azure have implemented their own Terraform providers that exclusively work with resources specific to them. For example, Azure provides the `"terraform-provider-azurerm"` provider. It exposes all the resources related to Azure that can be managed by Terraform using configuration files.

Figure 2-1 shows the Terraform architecture that can work with any remote API using the native provider and client library.

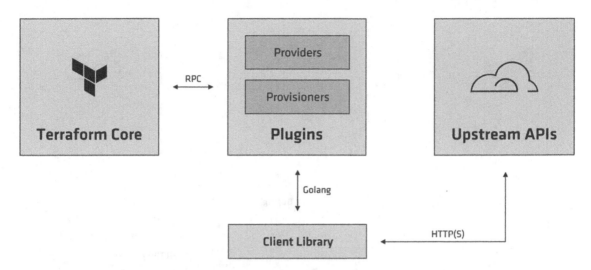

Figure 2-1. *Generic Terraform architecture*

Terraform interacts with the providers using remote procedure calls (RPCs). A Terraform script can have dependencies on multiple different providers, and Terraform will interact with all of them using RPC.

The Terraform providers are written in Golang as the SDK is implemented using Golang.

Figure 2-2 shows the Terraform architecture along with the remote Azure API that uses the Azure provider and client library.

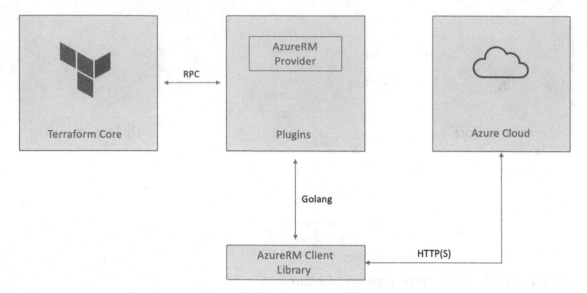

Figure 2-2. *Terraform architecture with Azure provider and client library*

The Azure cloud platform already has made its APIs publicly available for almost all its resources. There is a provider called `terraform-provider-azurerm` available along with its associated client library to enable Terraform to work with Azure resources and manage them.

It is always a good idea to understand the architecture of the software before installing and using it. Now that we understand the architecture at a high level, the next section will provide information about installing Terraform on local workstations.

Setting Up the Development Environment

Terraform installation can be as simple as downloading a single zip file and installing it by unzipping it to a folder. The zip file contains a single binary file. The folder should be added to the PATH environment variable such that the Terraform binary can be executed from command line without providing its complete path.

The advantage of manual installation is that the zip file is managed by Hashicorp, and the latest version is always available before any other method of installation. The download page has links for manual installation at `https://www.terraform.io/downloads.html`.

Terraform can also be downloaded and installed using the package manager available for each operating system.

To install Terraform on Windows using the Chocolatey package manager, use the command *choco install terraform* command.

To install Terraform on macOS using Homebrew, use the *brew install hashicorp/ tap/terraform* command. Before running the command, ensure that the Hashicorp repository is added using the command *brew tap hashicorp/tap*.

There are different package managers for each major Linux distribution. Debian has apt, RHEL has yum, and Fedora has dnf. Each of them should add the repository that consists of Terraform binaries and then install it using the install command. As an example, for an Ubuntu distribution, the command in Listing 2-1 can be used.

Listing 2-1. Commands for Installing Terraform on Ubuntu

```
curl -fsSL https://apt.releases.hashicorp.com/gpg | sudo apt-key add -

sudo apt-add-repository "deb [arch=amd64] https://apt.releases.hashicorp.
com $(lsb_release -cs) main"

sudo apt-get update && sudo apt-get install terraform
```

In addition to being available for Windows, Linux, and Mac, Terraform can be installed on Solaris, FreeBSD, and OpenBSD environments.

Terraform is available for both 32- and 64-bit processors, and you should download the appropriate binary based on your operating system and CPU architecture.

Note that there are no prerequisites to install Terraform. Although Terraform is implemented using the Golang language, Golang does not need to be installed as part of setting up a Terraform environment.

The Terraform website (https://www.terraform.io/downloads.html) provides an excellent guide to installing Terraform on different types of workstations.

Creating a Subscription with the Azure Cloud

This book uses Azure cloud as its target cloud environment. Therefore, it is necessary to have a valid subscription and access to the Azure cloud before we can execute the code provided with this book. Readers will get the maximum benefit from the book if they execute the book's code on an Azure subscription. The code can be executed on any valid Azure subscription.

If you do not have access to the Azure cloud, it can quickly be provisioned using the link https://azure.microsoft.com/en-in/free/.

Follow the steps provided by Microsoft to get access to the Azure subscription.

How Terraform Works

Terraform provides a command-line interface that accepts commands along with associated parameters. All interaction with Terraform happens using this CLI. Once Terraform is installed within a workstation, this CLI is available for execution (it should be added to the workstation's PATH environment variable). This CLI accepts commands. All the commands available from the CLI can be listed by executing the command "terraform" from a terminal window such as CMD in Windows or Bash in Linux and Mac.

These commands help in executing different flows such as initializing a Terraform environment, applying configurations in script files to the target environment, and many more. We will keep exploring these commands throughout this book. The commands in turn interact with the appropriate provider by passing in the resource configuration. The provider will use its client library to invoke the upstream APIs to update, delete, or read the resource configuration from the cloud infrastructure.

This is just a high-level explanation, and we will go into more detail about each of mentioned components starting next chapter.

Introducing State

As an astute reader, you might be wondering how Terraform understands whether it is a new environment—a configuration that has not yet executed before. How does it know if it should be creating new resources, updating existing resources, or ascertaining the current configuration of resources in cloud infrastructure? How does Terraform compare the configuration available locally in configuration files with that available in the remote cloud infrastructure?

The state file determines the action taken by Terraform on resources in the cloud infrastructure. But what is a state file?

A *state file* is a Terraform owned, text-based (JSON), dynamically generated file containing information about the resource configuration. It is generated by Terraform the first time a configuration file is executed in a working directory. Essentially, the state file is Terraform's view of the remote real-world infrastructure. It is a replica of the current state of resources in the cloud platform. When Terraform wants to compare and reconcile the configuration in the HCL scripts to resources in a cloud environment, it can do so by comparing the configuration directly with resources in cloud. Instead, it maintains a state file that has the current state of resources in the cloud, and it compares the configuration in an HCL script with the state file to determine whether it should create a new resource, update an existing resource, or delete and create a resource because the configuration drift is not compatible. It is the local representation in the current workspace of the configuration of resources in the target environment.

A state file is read and updated multiple times during different steps within each flow in Terraform. The different workflows and details about how and when a state file is used is covered in the next chapter.

To obtain mastery on Terraform, it is important to have the ability to write quality configuration files consisting of information related to providers and their resources, execute the commands with the appropriate parameters to manage the Terraform environment and target cloud environments. It is also important to understand the process of executing Terraform commands and deep dives into the architectural components of Terraform. This book will help provide this relevant information to enable readers to write enterprise-ready Terraform scripts for managing their cloud environment as well as managing Terraform itself.

Figure 2-3 shows the state file generated from the given configuration.

```
1    {
2      "version": 4,
3      "terraform_version": "0.13.0",
4      "serial": 6,
5      "lineage": "046c8189-1f44-d328-d6de-421c2b942e29",
6      "outputs": {
7 >     "resource_group_details": {-
36     },
37 >    "storage_account_details": {-
360    }
361    },
362    "resources": [
363      {
364        "mode": "managed",
365        "type": "azurerm_resource_group",
366        "name": "myrg",
367        "provider": "provider[\"registry.terraform.io/hashicorp/azurerm\"]",
368        "instances": [
369          {
370            "schema_version": 0,
371 >          "attributes": {-
377          },
378          "private":
             "eyJlMmJmYjczMC1lY2FhLTExZTYtOGY4OC0zNDM2M2JjN2M0YzAiOnsiY3JlYXRlIjo1NDAwMDAwMDAwMDAwLCJkZWxldGUiOjU0MDAwMDAwMDAwMDAsInJlYWQiOjMwMDAwMDAwMDAwM
             CwidXBkYXRlIjo1NDAwMDAwMDAwMDAwfX0="
379          }
380        ]
381      },
382      {
383        "mode": "managed",
384        "type": "azurerm_storage_account",
385        "name": "mystorage",
386        "provider": "provider[\"registry.terraform.io/hashicorp/azurerm\"]",
387        "instances": [
388          {
389            "schema_version": 2,
390 >          "attributes": {-
484          },
485          "private":
             "eyJlMmJmYjczMC1lY2FhLTExZTYtOGY4OC0zNDM2M2JjN2M0YzAiOnsiY3JlYXRlIjozNjAwMDAwMDAwMDAwLCJkZWxldGUiOjM2MDAwMDAwMDAwMDAsInJlYWQiOjMwMDAwMDAwMDAwM
             CwidXBkYXRlIjozNjAwMDAwMDAwMDAwfSwic2NoZW1hX3ZlcnNpb25pb24i0iIyIn0=",
486          "dependencies": [
487            "azurerm_resource_group.myrg"
488          ]
489          }
490        ]
491      }
492    ]
493  }
```

Figure 2-3. *Terraform state file*

Writing the First Terraform Configuration

Terraform provides the Hashicorp Configuration Language (HCL) to write Terraform
configurations. It is a simple language that helps to represent infrastructure resources in
text-based format with the .tf file extension. See Listing 2-2.

Listing 2-2. Terraform Configuration for Managing Resource Groups and
Storage Accounts in Azure

```
terraform {
    required_version = "~>v0.13.0"
    required_providers {
    azurerm = {
      version = "~> 2.36.0"
```

```
    source = "hashicorp/azurerm"
   }
  }
}

provider "azurerm" {
    features {}
}

variable resource_group_name {
    type = string
    description = "the name of resource group for containing resources"
}

variable resource_location {
    type = string
    description = "azure location for hosting resources"
}

variable storage_account_name {
    type = string
    description = "the name of Azure storage account"
}

resource "azurerm_resource_group" "myrg" {
  name     = var.resource_group_name
  location = var.resource_location
}

resource "azurerm_storage_account" "mystorage" {
  name                     = var.storage_account_name
  resource_group_name      = azurerm_resource_group.myrg.name
  location                 = azurerm_resource_group.myrg.location
  account_tier             = "Standard"
  account_replication_type = "LRS"

  tags = {
    environment = "test"
  }
}
```

```
resource "azurerm_resource_group" "myrg" {
  name     = var.resource_group_name
  location = var.resource_location
}

resource "azurerm_storage_account" "mystorage" {
  name                     = var.storage_account_name
  resource_group_name      = azurerm_resource_group.myrg.name
  location                 = azurerm_resource_group.myrg.location
  account_tier             = "Standard"
  account_replication_type = "LRS"

  tags = {
    environment = "test"
  }
}
output resource_group_details {
    value = azurerm_resource_group.myrg
}

output storage_account_details {
    value = azurerm_storage_account.mystorage
}
```

The configuration shown in the previous code will create a new Azure resource group and storage account with the name and at the location specified as part of values for variables while executing the configuration.

Let's get into a bit more detail about the configuration file. There is no top-level item in HCL. HCL configuration scripts are flat in nature, and there is no nesting of blocks in them. There are multiple block types such as "terraform", "variable", "provider", "resource", and "output" available that are used in the configuration. There are other blocks such as data, module, and locals available, and they will be introduced later in next chapter.

A `terraform` block is meant to configure Terraform behavior. A `terraform` block configures the following:

- Terraform's `required_version` binary version. All providers and modules should be able to work with the version provided in this block. There are multiple constraints that can be applied to versions, which will be explored in the chapter.

- The providers used within the configuration, via `required_providers`, along with their versions.

- The backend for the configuration (we will go into details of back ends in Chapter 3).

- Experimental feature configuration.

The `terraform` block declares its dependency on any version starting from Terraform version 0.13 but less than 0.14 version. This is configured using the `required_version` element. The block also has the `required_provider` element, which is responsible for setting up a local name for the provider along with its version and fully qualified name. The provider block listed after the terraform block should use this local name as the provider identifier. The `azurerm` name for the provider block matches the local name used in the Terraform block for the `azurerm` provider. If any of these configurations fails during the execution of the `init` command, the entire configuration will result in an error.

The provider is one of the important concepts in Terraform. Providers help extend Terraform with custom behavior, and all the cloud vendors including Azure have a provider to work with it. Each provider provides access to a collection of resource types. The `provider` block helps in configuring the provider behavior. The configuration shown earlier has a single provider element of type `azurerm`. We will go into further detail about provider configurations later; however, at this point, it has an empty `features` argument.

An empty `provider` block is optional if it was already mentioned in a `terraform` block. It should be used to add information such as authentication and back-end information.

Variables are placeholders in the configuration that accept external values as parameters during execution time. Variables help in authoring generic configurations and help in avoiding hard-coding within the script. Variables can be reused in almost all blocks within a configuration apart from `terraform` block, and we will see later why we cannot use variables within it. The variables declared in the shown configuration file in Listing 2-2 are needed to name the resource group and storage account and also set their locations.

The `resource` block relates to resources and their configurations to be managed by Terraform. The configuration in given example has just two resource elements. Each `resource` block represents a resource instance and is based on resource types available from the provider. There are two resource blocks: `azurerm_resource_group` and `azurerm_storage_account`. These are responsible for managing a resource group and storage account in Azure.

Readers might be intrigued that the previous explanation about resource types mentions managing the resource rather than provisioning or creating the resource. This is one of the fundamental concepts of infrastructure as code (IaC). The configuration just provides the definition and desired configuration for resources. In essence, it is providing information about "what" a resource should look like but not "how" a resource should be created and managed. Terraform decides during execution whether they should be provisioned, updated, deleted, or just left unchanged.

Lastly, there are couple of output blocks in the configuration file. These blocks help generate and return output values after evaluation of the expression's associated with them. The output in a current example is complete resource group and storage account configuration.

Applying a Terraform Configuration to Azure

Now that we have a Terraform configuration ready, we are going to execute it. We will be executing the configuration in multiple steps. The configuration needs values for three variables, which we will provide at execution time. Multiple commands should be executed in sequence to apply the configuration to target cloud platform.

These commands are executed in the context of folder containing all Terraform files. Terraform assumes the current folder/directory as a working directory if no explicit directory path is supplied in the context of executing these commands.

The general workflow to apply a Terraform configuration is depicted in Figure 2-4.

1. Initialize the Terraform working environment in a folder containing the configuration script.

2. Validate the configuration files for syntactical validity and consistency.

3. Refresh and reconcile the state file with the cloud infrastructure.

4. Generate the execution plan to check what will change in the target environment.

5. Apply the configuration to the target environment.

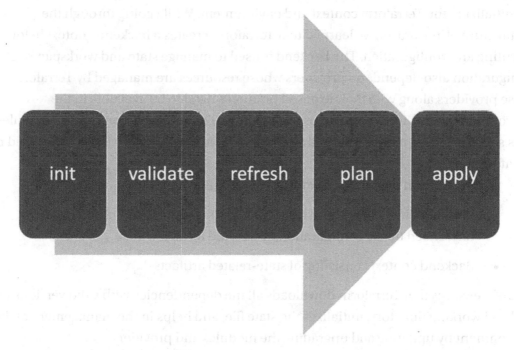

Figure 2-4. *Terraform activities in a workflow*

It is to be noted that the mentioned workflow is the simplest approach to apply a configuration to the target environment. There are many more minute details and additional steps in the workflow that we will witness while exploring advanced scenarios.

Initialize the Terraform Working Environment in a Folder Containing Configuration Files

Terraform provides command-line interface (CLI) commands that we can use to execute and manage the configuration and target cloud infrastructure. The CLI command executes the configuration files within the current folder context.

"init" is the first command that should be executed after authoring the Terraform script. init is the short form for "initialization," which means this command is used for initializing the Terraform context and environment. While going through the architecture of Terraform, we learned that Terraform creates a backend context before executing any configuration. The backend is used to manage state and workspaces. The configuration also depends on providers whose resources are managed by Terraform. These providers along with their exposed resources need to be available in the environment before Terraform can provision them. The configuration can use modules in its script, so these modules should also be available locally before they can be used by Terraform.

A valid Terraform environment consists of the following:

- Working directory comprising all providers (plugins) and modules referenced by the configuration files stored locally

- Backend context consisting of state-related artifacts

init ensures that Terraform downloads all the dependencies with valid versions in the local working directory, initializes the state file, and helps in the management of the environment by updating and upgrading the modules and providers.

Terraform's init command can be executed without supplying any flags explicitly, and in such cases, it uses the current working directory as its context. It accepts arguments as part of its execution, but all of them are optional.

Executing the `terraform init -help` command provides information about all the available flags.

The first configuration we wrote earlier uses a single provider (plugin) called azurerm. It does not have any dependency on any module. Also, since the configuration has not been executed yet, so there is no existing state.

The init command for our configuration should be able to download the azurerm provider and initialize the state in the current working directory. The init command creates a hidden .terraform folder and downloads the module and provider plugin in this hidden folder.

Executing the init command without any parameters as shown in Listing 2-3 will result in the initialization of the Terraform environment for our first configuration in the current working directory.

Listing 2-3. Terraform init Command Execution

```
Terraform init

Initializing the backend...

Initializing provider plugins...
- Finding latest version of hashicorp/azurerm...
- Installing hashicorp/azurerm v2.36.0...
- Installed hashicorp/azurerm v2.36.0 (signed by HashiCorp)

The following providers do not have any version constraints in
configuration, so the latest version was installed.

To prevent automatic upgrades to new major versions that may contain breaking
changes, we recommend adding version constraints in a required_providers
block in your configuration, with the constraint strings suggested below.

* hashicorp/azurerm: version = "~> 2.36.0"

Terraform has been successfully initialized!

You may now begin working with Terraform. Try running "terraform plan" to
see any changes that are required for your infrastructure. All Terraform
commands should now work.
```

If you ever set or change modules or backend configuration for Terraform, rerun this command to reinitialize your working directory. If you forget, other commands will detect it and remind you to do so if necessary.

As a result of the init command, the azurerm provider is download from the Hashicorp registry and stored in a folder structure, as shown in Listing 2-4. I am executing the init command on a Mac, so I got darwin_amd64 as a combination for the operating system and architecture name. The azurerm-provided version as of this writing was 2.35.0. This folder hierarchy is used on all platforms by Terraform. The OS and architecture name could differ from one OS to another.

Listing 2-4. Folder Structure After terraform init Command Execution

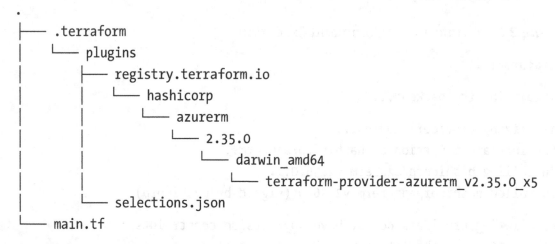

```
7 directories, 3 files
```

The init command performs certain validations specific to the provider and module configuration. If it finds an error during this validation check, the command fails. It will read the terraform and provider blocks from the configuration and validate them.

The terraform init command can be executed multiple times without any side effects.

Validate the Configuration Files for Syntactical Validity and Consistency

It is important to validate and check whether the configuration files within a working directory are syntactically correct, well-formed, and valid. It is possible to make different kinds of mistakes in configuration files, and a good process is to catch them before applying them in a real environment. It is a way to find errors in syntax early in the lifecycle so that appropriate corrective actions can be undertaken.

The command "`terraform validate`" helps in validating configuration files in a directory. To validate the configurations, Terraform should be aware of the declared plugins and modules, resources used from those plugins and modules, possible configurations for those resources, and the current state from the state file if available in the current workspace. The concepts related to modules will be covered in detail in Chapter 5.

The command `validate` can catch multiple error types like the following:

- Keywords usage and spelling

- Keywords not used as variable name

- Incorrect module name

- Interpolation usage where not allowed

- Missing quote in configuration

- Missing variable

- Valid output configuration

- Duplicate provider configuration

- Validate count value (should not be negative and should be valid integer value)

- Variable custom validation rules

- Duplicate module configuration

- Duplicate resource configuration

Executing the command `validate` as shown in Listing 2-5 with the previous configuration shows the successful result. In the case of an error, the same code will be displayed.

Listing 2-5. terraform validate Command Execution

```
terraform validate
Success! The configuration is valid.
```

The `terraform validate` command can be executed multiple times without any side effects.

Reconcile the Local State with the Remote Cloud Infrastructure Using the Refresh Command

The remote cloud infrastructure can undergo changes without Terraform being aware of it. Cloud platforms provide portals, APIs, and SDKs to help manage the infrastructure. Terraform should be made aware of the changes so that it can determine the actions and changes based on the actual drift between the configuration in the configuration files and the cloud infrastructure. The changes in the cloud infrastructure should be reflected in the state file since the last time the configuration executed to find the delta and drift. The job of the `refresh` command is to reconcile the local state with the remote cloud infrastructure.

The `refresh` command does not change the configuration files or cloud infrastructure. It changes and updates only the state file with the current configuration of the cloud infrastructure. This is an important point to note. The `refresh` command changes the state file if there is any drift between the existing configuration in the state file compared to the remote cloud infrastructure. Listing 2-6 shows the `refresh` command for the given configuration.

Listing 2-6. terraform refresh Command Execution

```
terraform refresh -var resource_group_name=simpleconfigrgname -var
resource_location="westeurope" -var storage_account_name=simpleterraformsto
reazure
```

If the `refresh` command is executed for the first time, as shown in Listing 2-7, it actually has nothing to refresh since the cloud infrastructure does not exist yet.

Listing 2-7. terraform refresh Command Execution Without Existing State File

```
terraform refresh -var resource_group_name=simpleconfigrgname -var
resource_location="westeurope" -var storage_account_
name=simpleterraformstoreazure
```

Empty or non-existent state file.

Refresh will do nothing. Refresh does not error or return an erroneous exit status because many automation scripts use refresh, plan, then apply and may not have a state file yet for the first run.

However, on subsequent execution, after the cloud infrastructure is deployed, as shown in Listing 2-8, executing the refresh command results in refreshing the state file.

Listing 2-8. terraform refresh Command Execution with Existing State File

```
terraform refresh -var resource_group_name=simpleconfigrgname -var
resource_location="westeurope" -var storage_account_
name=simpleterraformstoreazure

azurerm_resource_group.myrg: Refreshing state... [id=/
subscriptions/9755ffce-e94b-4332-9be8-1ade15e78909/resourceGroups/
simpleconfigrgname]
azurerm_storage_account.mystorage: Refreshing state... [id=/
subscriptions/9755ffce-e94b-4332-9be8-1ade15e78909/resourceGroups/
simpleconfigrgname/providers/Microsoft.Storage/storageAccounts/
simpleconfigrgname]

Outputs:

resource_group_details = {
  "id" = "/subscriptions/9755ffce-e94b-4332-9be8-1ade15e78909/
  resourceGroups/simpleconfigrgname"
  "location" = "westeurope"
  "name" = "simpleconfigrgname"
  "tags" = {}
}
....
```

The `terraform refresh` command can be executed without any flags just like the `init` command. The `refresh` command needs variable values, and they should be supplied by any of the available means in Terraform. We will have to supply the values for variables (if the configuration files do not have default values) declared within configuration files. The value for variables can be supplied using the `-var` option. Multiple `-var` options can be used, one for each declared variable. There is an alternate way to supply all the variable values in a config file and provide the file path using the `-var-file` option. The configuration shown before has three variable declarations, and the values for them are supplied using the `var` option, as shown here.

Note that using `-var` and `-var-file` is just one of the options to provide variable values to configuration variables. There are other means to supply the variable values, and in those cases, we do not need to use the `-var` and `-var-file` options. It is possible to declare environment variables or create a configuration file containing variable values like the `.tfvars` file to supply variable values. We will cover these techniques of supplying variable values in following chapters. The rules for suppling values for variables are the same for the `plan` and `apply` commands covered later in this chapter.

The `terraform refresh` command can change the state file, so it must be executed after careful consideration.

The `terraform refresh` command is again an optional step. Since it changes the state file, it is not used frequently. However, it is a good practice to use `refresh` as it displays the changes up front rather than later with other subsequent commands.

Generate the Execution Plan to Check What Will Change in the Target Environment

Once the Terraform environment's state has been initialized, the configuration files have been validated, and the state is updated, the next step is to execute the configuration files to provision or manage the resources on the remote cloud infrastructure. It is possible to apply the configuration to the target environment immediately after initialization and validation; however, it is always better to figure out the impact of executing the configuration files against the target environment. There are lots of things that can go wrong, and applying the configuration directly can result in an un-toward situation. It might put the target environment into a state that is not usable or makes applications go down.

The CLI plan command helps in "what-if" analysis related to configuration files in relation to the target cloud infrastructure. The plan command will reconcile the state file with the configuration of resources in the remote cloud infrastructure and then further compare the state file with the configurations in the working directory. Based on these stepwise comparisons, it is able to find the configuration drift between the configuration in the working directory and the real resources in the cloud infrastructure and provide feedback about whether a resource will be provisioned, deleted, replaced, updated in-place, or have no changes at all. As a result, it is also able to generate an execution plan containing the following details:

- Input variables and their values

- Output variables and whether they contain sensitive information

- Changes in resource configurations for each resource including both before and after configurations

- Action to be taken for each resource: create, update, delete, delete and update

- Changes in the output values compared to before and after applying the configuration

- Actual final configuration itself

plan command does not make any actual changes to the remote cloud infrastructure, the state file, or the configuration files. It generates a temporary updated state file to reconcile the differences with the current state of the remote cloud infrastructure and reverts to a previous known state after finding the configuration drift between the configurations. It is a way to evaluate the changes that might occur as a result of the actual application of configuration files to the target cloud infrastructure. Based on this feedback, the developer can decide whether it is prudent to apply the configuration or not.

The purpose of the `plan` command is to generate an execution plan that shows the drift between the configuration in the configuration files and the current state file.

Note that the `plan` command can be executed directly after the `init` command. The `plan` command will inherently validate the Terraform configuration as part of its execution.

Running the `terraform plan` command is an optional step; however, it's an important step to find what changes the configuration execution might have on the target environment. There are multiple implied substeps executed as part of executing a `plan` command. Executing a plan does the following:

- Loads the Terraform script and generates a graph of resources. This also includes resources declared within modules if a module is used in the configuration.

- Loads the current state file if it exists. A state file will not exist if a configuration has never been applied.

- Authenticates Terraform to the target environment (Azure in this case).

- Validates the configuration for syntactical correctness, validity, and well-formedness.

- If a state file exists, refreshes and generates a temporary state file to compare the differences between the actual configuration of resources in the target environment. It will not save the changes to the state file.

- Compares the resource configuration in the configuration files with the configuration of resources in the state files to generate an execution plan. The execution plan contains the actions and configuration changes Terraform will bring out if it is applied as part of the next step. Depending upon the findings, executing a plan does the following:

- Adds a resource if it exists in the configuration but does not exist in the state file.

- Updates a resource if it exists in both configurations, provided the configuration drift between them is compatible.

- Deletes and re-creates a resource if the configuration drift between a resource configuration is not compatible.

- Deletes a resource if it exists in the state file but the destroy option is applied.

- The resource configuration is unchanged otherwise.

Note that if a resource already exists in the target environment while the current state file does not contain information about it, the executing plan will result in an error if the same resource is also mentioned in the Terraform script. In such cases, the state for the resource under consideration should be imported prior to executing apply. The refresh does not import resources already in the target environment that do not exist in the state file. The refresh will just update the resource configuration in the state file with the resources available in the state file.

The terraform plan command can be executed without any flags just like the init command. There are multiple optional flags available with the plan command, however, we will have to supply the values for variables (if the variables do not have default values) declared within the configuration files. The value for variables can be supplied using the -var option, as shown in Listing 2-9. Multiple -var options can be used, one for each declared variable. There is an alternate way to supply all the variable values in a config file and provide the file path using the -var-file option. The configuration shown in Listing 2-X has three variable declarations, and the values for them are supplied using the var option, as shown in Listing 2-9.

Listing 2-9. terraform plan Command Execution

```
terraform plan -var resource_group_name=simpleconfigrg -var resource_
location="westeurope" -var storage_account_name=simpleterraformazure
```

Executing a Terraform plan generates an execution plan, as shown here:

```
terraform plan -var resource_group_name=simpleconfigrgname -var resource_
location="westeurope" -var storage_account_name=simpleterraformstoreazure
Refreshing Terraform state in-memory prior to plan...
The refreshed state will be used to calculate this plan, but will not be
persisted to local or remote state storage.

------------------------------------------------------------------------

An execution plan has been generated and is shown below.
Resource actions are indicated with the following symbols:
  + create

Terraform will perform the following actions:

  # azurerm_resource_group.myrg will be created
  + resource "azurerm_resource_group" "myrg" {
      + id       = (known after apply)
      + location = "westeurope"
      + name     = "simpleconfigrgname"
    }

  # azurerm_storage_account.mystorage will be created
  + resource "azurerm_storage_account" "mystorage" {
      + access_tier                      = (known after apply)
..
..
..
    }

Plan: 2 to add, 0 to change, 0 to destroy.

------------------------------------------------------------------------

Note: You didn't specify an "-out" parameter to save this plan, so
Terraform can't guarantee that exactly these actions will be performed if
"terraform apply" is subsequently run.
```

The `terraform plan` command can be executed multiple times without any side effects.

The generated execution plan can be saved to a file for later reuse, as shown in Listing 2-10. This execution plan can be used by the next step as input so that it does not generate the execution plan once again. The "out" option can be used for the file path for the newly generated execution plan.

Listing 2-10. terraform plan Command with Execution Plan File Generation

```
terraform plan -var resource_group_name=simpleconfigrgname -var resource_
location="westeurope" -var storage_account_name=simpleterraformstoreazure
-out=simpleconfig.tfplan
```

The previous command is similar to the `plan` command used earlier with the difference that an "out" option has been included in the new `plan` command. This will generate an execution plan and write it to `simpleconfig.tfplan` within the same working directory. This plan can be supplied as input to the "apply" command. The content of the execution plan can be converted into JSON and stored into another file for understanding the details of the plan using the `show` command, as shown in Listing 2-11.

Listing 2-11. Generating Terraform Execution Plan in Readable JSON Format

```
terraform show -json ./simpleconfig.tfplan >> readablesimpleconfig.json
```

The previous command takes the execution plan as input and generates a new file with JSON content in it. The new `readablesimpleconfig.json` can be opened using any text editor. Figure 2-5 shows the execution plan.

```
  1    {
  2        "format_version": "0.1",
  3        "terraform_version": "0.13.0",
  4        "variables": {
  5            "resource_group_name": { "value": "simpleconfigrgname" },
  6            "resource_location": { "value": "westeurope" },
  7            "storage_account_name": { "value": "simpleterraformstoreazure" }
  8        },
  9        "planned_values": {
 10            "outputs": {
 11                "resource_group_details": { "sensitive": false },
 12                "storage_account_details": { "sensitive": false }
 13            },
 14            "root_module": [...]
 56        },
 57        "resource_changes": [
 58            [...],
 76            [...]
147        ],
148        "output_changes": {
149            "resource_group_details": [...],
154            "storage_account_details": [...]
159        },
160        "configuration": {
161            "provider_config": [...],
167            "root_module": {
168                "outputs": [...],
172                "resources": [
173                    [...],
185                    [...]
201                ],
202                "variables": {
203                    "resource_group_name": { "description": "the name of resource group for containing resources" },
204                    "resource_location": { "description": "azure location for hosting resources" },
205                    "storage_account_name": { "description": "the name of Azure storage account" }
206                }
207            }
208        }
209    }
```

Figure 2-5. *Terraform execution plan in JSON format*

Apply the Configuration to the Target Environment Using the apply Command

The next step is to "apply" the configuration. The configuration can be executed and applied by running the CLI apply command. The apply command is similar to the plan command and follows the similar rules mentioned earlier with regard to its parameters. The values of variables should also be passed as part of the apply command.

Now that both the init and plan commands are already executed but they did not induce any changes to the target environment. We have yet to bring about any changes to the target environment and that is the responsibility of the apply command.

The apply command internally executes the validate and plan command before applying the configuration. This is an additional check performed by the apply command to check if anything further changed since the last execution of the plan command.

After performing the checks and generating an execution plan, the `apply` command asks for confirmation to continue as shown in Listing 2-12.

It uses the execution plan to apply the configuration to the remote cloud infrastructure and updates the state file simultaneously. If the configuration is run for the first time, the state file is generated otherwise, the state file is updated.

The `terraform apply` command can change both the remote cloud infrastructure and the state file and so it must be executed after careful consideration.

Listing 2-12. terraform apply Command Execution

```
terraform apply -var resource_group_name=simpleconfigrg -var resource_
location="westeurope" -var storage_account_name=simpleterraformazure

Plan: 2 to add, 0 to change, 0 to destroy.

Do you want to perform these actions?
  Terraform will perform the actions described above.
  Only 'yes' will be accepted to approve.

  Enter a value: yes

azurerm_resource_group.myrg: Creating...
azurerm_resource_group.myrg: Creation complete after 3s [id=/
subscriptions/9755ffce-e94b-4332-9be8-1ade15e78909/resourceGroups/
simpleconfigrgname]
azurerm_storage_account.mystorage: Creating...
azurerm_storage_account.mystorage: Still creating... [10s elapsed]
azurerm_storage_account.mystorage: Still creating... [20s elapsed]
azurerm_storage_account.mystorage: Still creating... [30s elapsed]
azurerm_storage_account.mystorage: Creation complete after 32s [id=/
subscriptions/9755ffce-e94b-4332-9be8-1ade15e78909/resourceGroups/
simpleconfigrgname/providers/Microsoft.Storage/storageAccounts/
simpleconfigrgname]

Apply complete! Resources: 2 added, 0 changed, 0 destroyed.
```

```
Outputs:

resource_group_details = {
  "id" = "/subscriptions/9755ffce-e94b-4332-9be8-1ade15e78909/
  resourceGroups/simpleconfigrgname"
  "location" = "westeurope"
  "name" = "simpleconfigrgname"
}
storage_account_details = {
  "access_tier" = "Hot"
  "account_kind" = "StorageV2"
..
 }
}
```

After the apply command successfully completes, it maintains the generated state file named terraform.tfstate in the working directory. This is the default name and location for the state file and can be overridden using the -state option.

Listing 2-13 shows the new folder structure after applying the configuration. Notice the newly created terraform.tfstate file.

Listing 2-13. Folder Structure After Execution of the apply Command

```
.
├── .terraform
│   └── plugins
│       ├── registry.terraform.io
│       │   └── hashicorp
│       │       └── azurerm
│       │           └── 2.35.0
│       │               └── darwin_amd64
│       │                   └── terraform-provider-azurerm_v2.35.0_x5
│       └── selections.json
├── main.tf
└── terraform.tfstate

7 directories, 4 files
```

It is important to note that both the plan and apply commands lock the state file to ensure that it can be modified by a single user at a time. Once a user has completed the command execution, the lock is released for use by the next user.

It is evident from the previous description that apply by default executes many commands that were also executed explicitly. If a plan file is provided to apply command, it will not perform any further validation. It will not even require the values for variables since these are already part of the execution plan.

To execute the apply command in conjunction with an already existing plan, run the command as shown in Listing 2-14.

Listing 2-14. terraform apply Command Execution Using an Existing Execution Plan

```
terraform apply ./simpleconfig.tfplan
```

This time Terraform does not execute the validate and plan steps or ask for confirmation to apply the configuration. It starts by applying the configuration directly to the remote cloud infrastructure.

```
azurerm_resource_group.myrg: Creating...
azurerm_resource_group.myrg: Creation complete after 2s [id=/
subscriptions/9755ffce-e94b-4332-9be8-1ade15e78909/resourceGroups/
simpleconfigrg]
azurerm_storage_account.mystorage: Creating...
azurerm_storage_account.mystorage: Still creating... [10s elapsed]
azurerm_storage_account.mystorage: Still creating... [21s elapsed]
azurerm_storage_account.mystorage: Still creating... [31s elapsed]
azurerm_storage_account.mystorage: Still creating... [41s elapsed]
azurerm_storage_account.mystorage: Creation complete after 48s [id=/
subscriptions/9755ffce-e94b-4332-9be8-1ade15e78909/resourceGroups/
simpleconfigrg/providers/Microsoft.Storage/storageAccounts/simpleconfigrg]

Apply complete! Resources: 2 added, 0 changed, 0 destroyed.
```

```
Outputs:

resource_group_details = {
  "id" = "/subscriptions/9755ffce-e94b-4332-9be8-1ade15e78909/
          resourceGroups/simpleconfigrg"
  "location" = "westeurope"
  "name" = "simpleconfigrg"
}
storage_account_details = {
  "access_tier" = "Hot"
  "account_kind" = "StorageV2"
..
  }
}
```

Although using a `.tfplan` file directly is a good idea to reuse an already generated plan because it lessens the possibility of error, it might be possible that the execution plan has become old and might not reflect a true execution plan. This could be because the target cloud infrastructure might have undergone changes since the time the last execution plan was generated.

We can reuse an old execution plan if there is tight governance and management of cloud access and resources do not allow manual changes and all changes happen using the Terraform configuration. It is also possible to generate a new execution plan every time configuration files need to be applied to the target cloud infrastructure and to use the new plan with the `apply` command. This reduces the risk that the execution plan has become outdated because of resources in the cloud infrastructure changing.

Figure 2-6 summarizes all the commands and their relationships along with their flow. The first step is to initialize and then execute the commands `validate`, `refresh`, `plan`, and `apply`. The command `plan` can be executed directly without executing the `validate` and `refresh` commands, and `apply` can be executed directly after the `init` command.

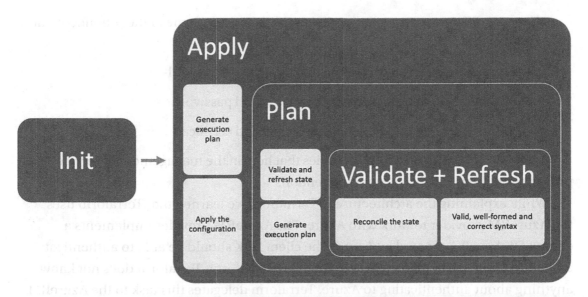

Figure 2-6. Terraform commands and their relationships

Segregating each functionality into separate commands helps a developer validate the configuration scripts locally before pushing the code to a repository or raising a pull request to submit changes. Developers can execute the init, refresh, validate, and plan commands to check the impact of changes on the remote cloud environment before raising their pull request to merge the code to the main repository. The pipelines executed in response to accepting the pull request can revalidate the configuration scripts using the same commands before merging the code.

The deployment pipelines can again re-validate and execute the apply command to bring changes to the lower environments before making changes to the production environment. Chapter 7 covers how multiple team members can collaborate while using Terraform along with CI/CD pipelines and remote state.

Terraform Authentication to Azure

Azure implements OpenID connect and oAuth for the authentication and authorization of requests. Azure Active Directory is the main service that implements these protocols and provides authorization and token endpoints needed within the oAuth and OpenID connect flows. Using these endpoints, it is possible to adopt oAuth authorization flow, client-credentials flow, and implicit flow. These different flows can use password or certificates as a means of authenticating with Azure AD.

There are different ways to authenticate with Azure AD. Some of the prominent ones are as follows:

- Authenticating using a simple username and password

- Authenticating using a service principal and password

- Authenticating using a service principal and certificate

Azure also provides managed identities that help in the management of service principals without any direct user intervention.

While explaining the architecture of Terraform, we learned that Terraform uses the AzureRM provider to work with Azure. The AzureRM provider implements a client SDK for APIs exposed by Azure. The client SDK should be able to authenticate and authorize itself to manage resources using Terraform. Terraform does not know anything about authenticating to Azure. Terraform delegates this task to the AzureRM provider, and it is the responsibility of the provider to get authenticated to Azure using the client SDK. However, Terraform has a role to play in the authentication process. It should be able to send the credential information to the provider. Again, there are multiple ways Terraform can obtain credentials needed by the provider to authenticate to Azure.

- Authenticating using the Azure CLI

- Authenticating using the service principal and client secret

- Authenticating using the service principal and client certificate

- Authenticating using managed identities

In this chapter, we will use the simplest authentication and authorization method, i.e., authentication using the Azure CLI with user credentials.

Authentication Using the Azure CLI

To authenticate to Azure using the az CLI command with user credentials, open a terminal window and execute the command as shown in Listing 2-15.

Listing 2-15. Logging in to Azure Using the az CLI Login Command

```
Az login
```

This will open a new browser window asking the user to log in to Azure with their credentials. Once the user is logged in, the terminal window will list all the subscriptions that the user has access to, and it can select one of subscriptions using the command shown in Listing 2-16.

Listing 2-16. Selecting a Valid Azure Subscription

```
Az account set -s "xxxxxxx-xxxx-xxxxx-xxxxxxxxxxxx"
```

Here, the `"s"` parameter expects a subscription ID, or a subscription name.

Now using the terminal, Terraform commands can be executed, and the remote cloud infrastructure will be managed in the subscription selected earlier.

List of Terraform Commands Used in This Chapter

Listing 2-17 shows all the Terraform commands used in this chapter. The commands remain the same in subsequent deployments. You should be careful when using commands that bring about change to the state file and the remote cloud infrastructure and only execute them after careful evaluation of the execution plan.

Listing 2-17. Terraform Commands Used in This Chapter for Applying Configurations to the Azure Cloud

```
terraform init

terraform validate

terraform refresh -var resource_group_name=simpleconfigrgname
-var resource_location="westeurope" -var storage_account_
name=simpleterraformstoreazure
```

```
terraform plan -var resource_group_name=simpleconfigrgname -var resource_
location="westeurope" -var storage_account_name=simpleterraformstoreazure
```

```
terraform apply -var resource_group_name=simpleconfigrgname -var resource_
location="westeurope" -var storage_account_name=simpleterraformstoreazure
```

Summary

This was the first chapter where we really got to know Terraform closely. In this chapter, Terraform was introduced, its architecture and important components were discussed. The chapter started with a discussion of the Terraform architecture followed by an introduction to the state files. The steps to install Terraform on different platforms were briefly mentioned, which led to authoring our first Terraform configuration. After writing the configuration file, it has to be applied to the remote cloud platform. This was done in a series of steps starting with the `init` command followed by the `validate`, `refresh`, `plan`, and `apply` commands. Each command adds value to the process by demonstrating its behavior either by checking the configuration syntax (`validate`), reconciling the local state with remote cloud state (`refresh`), generating an execution plan (`plan`), or applying the configuration (`apply`). There are multiple ways to authenticate to Azure from Terraform, and this chapter used user credentials along with the Azure CLI. The next chapter will cover the individual commands with an introduction to the back end. We'll also write some more configurations on Azure.

CHAPTER 3

Getting Started with Terraform

The previous two chapters introduced the foundational concepts related to infrastructure as code (IaC) and also introduced Terraform architecture. This chapter will go into some of the important elements of writing Terraform scripts. This chapter will focus on variables, variable datatypes, providers, outputs, remote state, and file/folder layout for writing Terraform scripts.

Terraform Variables

Variables are an important concept in Terraform. They accept external values and help in authoring generic scripts. Terraform provides variable blocks, and there can be multiple such blocks in a script. Each block represents a single variable. The syntax of a variable consists of a variable keyword followed by a variable name. The variable name should be unique within a script. The block followed by the name consists of multiple attributes. The important one is the type attribute, and it represents the datatype of the variable. A variable declaration is shown here:

```
Variable resourceGroupName {
    Type= string
}
```

A variable can have a default value. This default value is used in case external value for variable is missing during execution.

```
Variable resourceGroupName {
    Type= string
    Default = "dev-ecommerce-rg"
}
```

© Ritesh Modi 2021
R. Modi, *Deep-Dive Terraform on Azure*, https://doi.org/10.1007/978-1-4842-7328-9_3

There is also description attribute that helps provide a textual description about the usage of the variable. It is a good practice to provide a description to every variable. It helps the reader of the script easily understand its usage.

```
Variable resourceGroupName {
    Type= string
    Default = "dev-ecommerce-rg"
    Description = "This is used for naming the resource group related to
    ecommerce application in development environment"
}
```

Version 0.13 of Terraform added a new validation attribute. Since the values are supplied externally, it is quite possible that the value is within a constrained range, specific value or meet certain conditions. The validation attribute helps in validating the input value and would execute the script only if the validation passes successfully.

```
variable rgname {
    type = string
    validation {
        condition = (length(var.rgname) <= 90 && length(var.rgname) > 2 &&
        can(regex("[-\\w\\._\\(\\)]+", var.rgname)) )
        error_message = "Resource group name may only contain alphanumeric
        characters, dash, underscores, parentheses and periods."
    }
}
```

The validation condition necessitates that the resource group name should be between 2 and 90 characters long and should contain only alphanumeric characters, dashes, underscores, parentheses, and periods. The validation condition makes use of Terraform functions, which will be covered in the next chapter.

The error_message should start with a capital letter and must end either with a period or with a question mark.

Version 0.14 of Terraform added an additional "sensitive" attribute to the variable block. It accepts Boolean true/false values, and setting it to true will ensure that the value will not be displayed using the Terraform CLI.

```
variable rgname {
    type = string
    validation {
        condition = (length(var.rgname) <= 90 && length(var.rgname) > 2 &&
        can(regex("[-\\w\\._\\(\\)]+", var.rgname)) )
        error_message = "Resource group name may only contain alphanumeric
        characters, dash, underscores, parentheses and periods."
    }
    sensitive = true
}
```

Understanding Terraform Datatypes

As shown in the previous section, Terraform variables help you write generic scripts and help you customize the scripts without changing the code. Terraform variables support multiple datatypes, as shown here:

- string: This is a simple datatype that accepts alphanumeric characters along with special characters.

- bool: This is a simple datatype that accepts binary true/false values.

- number: This is a simple datatype that accepts a series of numbers.

- object: This is a complex structural type that accepts a series of key-value pairs. It consists of multiple simple and other complex types, and they together can be represented using a single variable. The keys in the object datatype are not arbitrary, and they do need to conform to type declaration.

- map: This is a complex collection type that accepts a series of key-value pairs. Each value should be of the same type as defined during the declaration. For example, values for the map(number) datatype can have numerical data only for its number value. In other programming languages, it is known as the dictionary datatype.

45

The keys in the `map` datatype are arbitrary, and they do not need to conform to any declaration.

- `list`: This is a complex collection type and accepts a series of values. This datatype does not have keys; instead, it has a numerical index starting from 0. Each value should be of the same type as defined during the declaration. In other programming languages, it is quite similar to the `array` datatype. For example, the values for the `list(bool)` datatype can have Boolean `true`/`false` data only for its value.

- `tuple`: This datatype is similar to the `list` datatype. It is a complex collection type and accepts a series of values, with each having a numerical value assigned in an index starting from 0. Each value can be of a different type as defined during the declaration. For example, `tuple([string, number, bool])` can accept alphanumeric, numerical, and Boolean data in this order. The ordering is an important nature of the `tuple` datatype.

- `sets`: This datatype is a complex collection type and accepts a series of unique values. This datatype does not have keys or an index. It does not have a secondary identifier at all. Each value should be a different type as defined during the declaration. Sets do not have any ordering, and the only requirement is that all values must be unique.

- `any`: The `any` datatype is a symbolic datatype and does not represent any particular datatype. Using it means that the datatype will be determined at runtime rather at design time. At runtime, depending on the value, the type will be ascertained.

Working with Lists

Lists are a collection of values that are accessed using a numerical index and they consist of values of a similar type. The next code listing contains a variable named `listofstrings` of type `list(string)`. It means it is a collection of `string` values. The default value is provided as a `string` collection. The `listofstrings` output block outputs all the values stored within the list, and the `singlevaluefromlistofstrings` outputs generates a single value as Output from the collection using a numerical index of 1. The first index value is 0, so the output provides 2 as its value.

```
variable listofstrings {
    type = list(string)
    default = ["one", "two", "three", "four"]
}

Output listofstrings {
    Value  = var.listofstrings
}

Output singlevaluefromlistofstrings {
    Value = var.listofstrings[1]
}
```

The next code listing is different from the previous listing. The datatype is a list of the "any" type. This means the list can consist of any values provided they all are of the same type. In the code listing, all literal values mentioned as default will be converted to strings values.

```
variable listofhybriditems {
    type = list(any)
    default = [10, "ritesh", true, "modi"]
}

Output listofhybriditems  {
    Value  = var.listofhybriditems
}

Output singlevaluefromlistofhybriditems  {
    Value = var.listofhybriditems[1]
}
```

The next code listing shows an example of a list of map datatypes. The map in turn contains only values of type string. The default value consists of a list of maps. Each map comprises a two key-value pair: name and age. The values for both name and age are of type string.

```
variable listofmaps {
    type = list(map(string))
    default  = [
        {
            name = "ritesh"
            age = "20"
        },
        {
            name = "avni"
            age = "10"
        }
    ]
}
```

The next code listing shows an example of a list of object datatypes. The object in turn comprises two elements: the location of type string and the age of type number.

```
variable listofobjects {
    type = list(object({
        location = string
        age = number
    }
    ))
    default  = [
        {
            location = "hyderabad"
            age = 20
        },
        {
            location = "kolkata"
            age = 10
        },
```

```
    {
        location = "bangalore"
        age = 30
        name = "ritesh"
    }
  ]
}
```

Working with Maps

Maps are collection types in Terraform that are inherently implemented as dictionaries. They are key-value pairs with the condition that each key should be unique within the collection, and all values should adhere to the data type specified during declaration time. The code listing shown next defines a variable of type map(string). The values for each of the keys should be of the string type.

```
variable mymapstring {
    type = map(string)
    default = {
        "key1" = "value1"
        "key2" = "value2"
        "key3" = "value 3"
    }
}
```

Accessing a map is through the usage of the key. They key determines the individual value to be accessed, as shown next:

```
output mymapoutputwhole {
    value = var.mymapstring
}

output mymapoutputone {
    value = var.mymapstring["key2"]
}
```

A map can also be declared with "any" datatype, as shown next:

```
variable mymapany {
    type = map(any)
    default = {
        "key1" = "value1"
        "key2" = 10
        "key3" = false
    }
}
```

Working with Objects

Objects, as we already know by now, are structural types in Terraform and closely represent JSON objects. They help in grouping multiple simple and complex types together as a single type. The next listing shows a variable definition with myEmployeeObject of type object. It has five elements: name, age, is_married, companies, and schools. Each of them is of a different data type, namely, string, number, bool, map(string), and list(string), respectively. The default value shows the object with the values.

```
variable myEmployeeObject {
    type = object({
        name = string
        age = number
        is_married = bool
        companies = map(string)
        schools = list(string)
    })
    default = {
        name = "ritesh"
        age = 25
        is_married = true
        companies = {
            "company1" = "abcd"
```

```
        "2company" = "xyz"
    }
    schools = ["school1", "school2"]
}

}
```

The next code listing has another variable called myEmployeeAny defined with the same elements as the previous variables. The only difference is the use of the "any" datatype rather than specific data types. In this case, each element can accept any value, and the datatype will be coerced to a type depending on the value at runtime.

```
variable myEmployeeAny {
    type = object({
        name = any
        age = any
        is_married = any
        companies = any
        schools = any
    })
    default = {
        name = "ritesh"
        age = 25
        is_married = true
        companies = {
            "company1" = "abcd"
            "2company" = "10"
        }
        schools = ["school1", "school2"]
    }

}
```

Working with Sets

Sets are collections that can contain only unique values of the same datatype with no specified ordering. They also cannot be accessed using indexing.

The code listing shown next has three different variable declarations. The first myset variable defines a set of type string. This means it can contain unique string values with no specified ordering. The second variable, mysetany, defines a set of type any. The default value contains all the elements of the numerical type, so its data type is regarded as a number at runtime. If there are values of different data types specified, then all of them are converted to strings if there is a string literal present within all the specified values, as shown with the usage of the third, mysethybrid variable.

```
variable myset {
    type = set(string)
    default = ["one", "two", "three", "four", "two"]
}

variable mysetany {
    type = set(any)
    default = [10,20,30,40, 30]
}

//converts every element to string
variable mysethybrid {
    type = set(any)
    default = [10, "ritesh", true, "modi"]
}
```

The next code listing shows how to use a "set" collection type along with the "map" collection type:

```
variable setofmaps {
    type = set(map(string))
    default  = [
        {
            name = "ritesh"
            age = "20"
        },
```

```
    {
        name = "avni"
        age = "10"
    }
  ]
}
```

The next code listing shows how to use a `"set"` collection type along with the `"object"` structural type:

```
variable setofobjects {
    type = set(object({
        location = string
        age = number
    }
    ))
    default  = [
        {
            location = "hyderabad"
            age = 20
        },
        {
            location = "kolkata"
            age = 10
        },
        {
            location = "bangalore"
            age = 30
            name = "ritesh"
        }
    ]
}
```

It is important to note that there is no direct way to access values in a set. A set can be accessed as a whole directly by referring to it by its name; however, to fetch individual values from a set, the set should first be converted into a list before using it, as shown next:

```
value = tolist(var.myset)[0]
```

Working with Tuples

Tuples are structural types in Terraform and quite similar to the list collection type. Tuples can be accessed using an index; however, each piece of data within a tuple can be of different data type. It does not have any key value as in the case of dictionary or map collection types.

The next code listing shows a simpletuple variable definition comprising three different primitive types: string, number, and bool. The values accepted should be in similar order according to order of specified data types. The individual values can be accessed using index notation starting from 0.

```
variable simpletuple {
    type = tuple([string, number, bool])
    default = ["ritesh", 10, false]
}
```

Providers

Terraform scripts and modules are dependent on providers to operate on target cloud platform. This was explained in detail in the previous chapter while discussing the architecture of Terraform. Terraform provides a provider block that helps in configuring the dependency on the provider and also its configuration. Version 0.13 introduced a new block called required-providers within the terraform block. It does the same job as the provider block and is the recommended way to declare a dependency on a provider. Note that both the provider and required_providers blocks are supported, and the provider configuration should be supplied in the provider configuration, while the version and source should be used within the required_providers block.

```
terraform {
    required_providers {
        azurerm = {
            source  = "hashicorp/azurerm"
            version = "~> 2.41"
        }
    }
}

provider azurerm {
    features {}
}

resource azurerm_resource_group rg {
    name= "providertestrg"
    location = "west europe"
}
```

In the previous code listing, the source is hashicorp/azurerm, which is a short form to accessing the provider plugin. The full URI is shown in the next code listing. All Terraform-approved and curated provider plugins are hosted at registry. terraform.io.

The URI can be broken into three parts: HOST, NAMESPACE, and Type.

The host refers to the location hosting the provider. The host can have multiple namespaces, with Hashicorp being the default namespace, and each namespace can host multiple provider types.

Versioning

Each Terraform provider has its own development and release lifecycle along with different version number as it continues to evolve. The version number is specified within the required_providers block for each provider using the "version" attribute.

Terraform uses semantic versioning for providers. The versioning scheme is broken into major, minor, and patch number. Major version changes involve breaking changes from the previous version. Minor version changes involve changes that do not break previous version functionality but will fix bugs and allow additional features. Patch version changes are primarily bug fixes.

Terraform uses versioning constraints to specify the provider versions using semantic versioning.

The next code listing uses an exact match for the version number. In such cases, the provider version used will be 2.41.0 for every execution of the script.

```
azurerm = {
    source  = "registry.terraform.io/hashicorp/azurerm"
    version = "=2.41.0"
}
```

It is also possible to use the >, <, and != operators with version numbers. The next code listing shows using a version number greater than 2.39.0. At the time of writing this chapter, the version is 2.41.0.

```
terraform {
    required_providers {
        azurerm = {
            source  = "registry.terraform.io/hashicorp/azurerm"
            version = ">2.39.0"
        }
    }
}
```

Similarly, it is possible to install a version that is greater than or equal to a specified version number. The next code listing installs version 2.41.0 at the time of writing. You might notice a different version getting installed.

```
terraform {
    required_providers {
        azurerm = {
            source  = "registry.terraform.io/hashicorp/azurerm"
            version = ">=2.39.0"
        }
    }
}
```

It is also possible to provide multiple conditions separated by a comma, as shown in the next code listing:

```
terraform {
    required_providers {
        azurerm = {
            source  = "registry.terraform.io/hashicorp/azurerm"
            version = ">2.39.0, <2.41.0"

        }
    }
}
```

Terraform also provides the ~ operator for determining the provider version number. The ~ operator is special because it constrains the version number within a range depending upon the format of the version number specified. The next code listing uses a three-part version number: 2.39.0. In this case, the latest version starting with 2.39.0 up to a version that does not switch over to 2.40 is used. ~ works with the > or >= operator only. The next code listing will install the 2.39.x version.

```
terraform {
    required_providers {
        azurerm = {
            source  = "registry.terraform.io/hashicorp/azurerm"
            version = "~>2.39.0"

        }
    }
}
```

The code listing shown next will result into an error because it is incorrect since it uses the = operator, which is not supported by the ~ operator.

```
terraform {
    required_providers {
        azurerm = {
            source  = "registry.terraform.io/hashicorp/azurerm"
            version = "~=2.39.0"

        }
    }
}
```

The next code listing uses a two-part version number, including the major and minor numbers. In such a case, the version number will not reach version 3, and anything lower than 3.0 will be downloaded. As of this writing, this provider configuration downloads version 2.41.0.

```
terraform {
    required_providers {
        azurerm = {
            source  = "registry.terraform.io/hashicorp/azurerm"
            version = "~>2.39"

        }
    }
}
```

The next code listing is invalid as it uses the less-than (<) operator:

```
terraform {
    required_providers {
        azurerm = {
            source  = "registry.terraform.io/hashicorp/azurerm"
            version = "~<2.39"

        }
    }
}
```

It is also possible to use multiple conditions separated by a comma using the ~ operator.

```
terraform {
    required_providers {
        azurerm = {
            source  = "registry.terraform.io/hashicorp/azurerm"
            version = "~>2.36, ~>2.40"

        }
    }
}
```

Multiproviders

It is also possible to declare multiple providers and use them within resources referring to them by their name. The next code listing declares two required_providers blocks: one with azurerm and the other as someotherprovider. The configuration for both the providers in the provider block could be different. One provider could be connected to one subscription, while the other provider could be connected to another subscription. This scenario is quite common when you want to configure a peer-to-peer virtual network connection between subscriptions.

```
terraform {
    required_providers {
        azurerm = {
            source  = "registry.terraform.io/hashicorp/azurerm"
            version = "~>2.36, ~>2.40"

        }
        someotherprovider = {
            source  = "registry.terraform.io/hashicorp/azurerm"
            version = "~>2.36, ~>2.40"

        }
    }
}
```

```
provider azurerm {
    features {}
}

provider someotherprovider  {
    features {}
}

resource azurerm_resource_group rg {
    name= "providertestrg"
    location = "west europe"
    provider = someotherprovider
}
```

Outputs

Terraform takes inputs in the form of variables and provisions resources using resource blocks. It can also output values using the output block. Each output block generates output that is displayed on the execution console after the script has finished its execution. There can be multiple output blocks in a Terraform script. Each output block starts with the "output" keyword followed by its name. Each output block has a value attribute that determines the value to generate and output from the script. The value on the right of this attribute could be a literal value or an expression that will be evaluated at runtime to generate the output.

Although it is a good practice to output values from Terraform scripts to the console, an important aspect of outputs is to supply these dynamic output values to other Terraform scripts that might be dependent on these values. This way, it is possible to chain multiple Terraform scripts and pass dynamic values from one to another and make these scripts modular and generic as well.

State Management in Terraform

Terraform stores the state of deployments in a state file. The state file contains a resource configuration as seen and understood by Terraform from its last run. It is a way for Terraform to represent the current resources and configuration available on the target platform. The state file is generated while executing the Terraform script, and by default it is generated in a local folder in the context of the execution path. State files are essential for have Terraform work correctly.

We executed a Terraform script in the previous chapter, and it generated a state file. It is important to understand that generating a state file on a local machine is a valid option if that is the only available machine used by a single developer. In such a scenario, the developer has access to a state file and can repeatedly execute the scripts without any issues. The problem starts to arise as soon as there are multiple developers working on the same script or executing the same scripts from different locations. There should just be one instance of the state file for an environment, and Terraform will not have information about it if the script is executed from a new location. This can lead to multiple issues.

- Multiple teams and developers cannot collaborate on the same Terraform scripts and execution unless the state file is physically copied by developers. The precondition for a state file to be used within a team by multiple developers is that there should be a single state file (this condition is already met by Terraform), and it should be sharable (this condition is not met by Terraform by default).

- The execution of Terraform scripts is tied to a single machine unless the state file is physically copied to other environments. This again can impose significant challenges. If the machine is not available for any reason, then an alternate machine with a backup copy of the state is the only way to further execute the Terraform scripts. It is for these reasons state file should not be stored locally but to a central location and multiple developers can all refer to this central location as a reference to state file while working with local Terraform scripts.

There are multiple configuration changes that should be applied before a state file can be shared and used by developers as a team. Terraform supports local state as witnessed in the previous chapter. It also supports remote state. Storing a state file at a central location that can be accessed and referenced from local Terraform scripts is known as *remote state*.

a. The state file should be stored in a location that is accessible from the developer's local Terraform scripts. This location can be any location reachable from a developer's workstation supported by Terraform.

b. After identifying a central location for state files, this new information should be made available to Terraform scripts such that they can utilize it to generate the state file at this central location rather than locally from a place of execution.

There can be multiple locations where state files can reside. Important is that Terraform should be able to retrieve, save, update, delete, or migrate state files from these locations. Some of the major ones supported by Terraform are:

- *Azure*: State can be stored in Azure storage accounts. They are highly secure, available, and fault tolerant by default and can be accessed using the HTTP/S protocol from the Internet as well as the local network.

- *Etcdv2 and Etcdv3*: These are distributed key-value stores with high reliability, availability, and consistency.

- *Kubernetes*: This is a highly secure, reliable, and scalable orchestrator for managing containers on any platform and cloud. State files can be stored.

- *Google and Amazon cloud storage accounts*: The state files can be stored in any cloud storage including Google storage and Amazon S3 accounts.

- *Consul*: It is supported by Hashicorp and provides a key-value store similar to ETCD with high reliability, availability, and consistency.

- *HTTP*: Using this remote-state type, it is possible to use the REST protocol to work with state files.

There are more types of remote state supported by Terraform including artifactory, pg and OSS.

Terraform provides a CLI that accepts multiple commands, and each command performs an action. The action might access, read, and optionally update the state file. Local state supports all commands and actions using the CLI, while remote state supports all the important commands except the Refresh command. The Refresh command is not available for remote state.

It is important that remote state is a secure location since the state file can contain sensitive information that should not get compromised. We will look into this aspect in greater detail in chapter related to Terraform security later in the book.

Each remote-state type provides its own means for authentication from Terraform. Terraform can securely authenticate and connect to Azure storage accounts using a Service Principal, Managed identity, SAS tokens or storage keys. The Azure storage hosted state file can be accessed using the following:

- *A service principal*: A Service Principal along with either a secret or certificate can be used to authenticate to storage account using role based access control policies in Azure. A service principal is managed using Azure AD.

- *Managed identity*: A managed identity is similar to a service principal managed by Azure AD. It also uses role based access control to access the state file stored in storage account.

- *Storage access key*: Each storage account has a set of unique keys available to them. The storage accounts can be accessed by anyone possessing these Keys. These keys are not part of Azure AD.

- *Shared access signature (SAS) token*: Each storage account allows generation of multiple tokens allowing differential access to items within the storage account. The storage services and items can be accessed by anyone possessing these tokens. A SAS token can be generated with granular permissions, valid within a date range, and can be revoked at any time.

Setting Up Remote State for Terraform Deployments

As mentioned earlier, two steps should be executed to store and manage state in Azure remote state. The storage account along with SAS token would be provisioned using Terraform and it would require a complete Terraform configuration including providers, resources, variables and outputs.

Provision of Remote Azure Storage Infrastructure

This step involves provisioning a new Azure storage account (V2), provisioning a container to host the state file, and generating a SAS token. This information will then be used in the next step. Terraform can be used to provision the Azure remote-state infrastructure.

The code listing shown next does the following:

- Provisions a resource group

- Provisions a storage account

- Provisions a container within a storage account

- Generates a storage account SAS token

- Generates a storage account container SAS token

- Outputs both the generated SAS token

Configuring the azurerm Provider

We will start by configuring the azurerm provider. features is the only required attribute, and it is a good practice to mention the version number.

```
provider "azurerm" {
    version = "~>2.0"
    features {}
}
```

Next, we will create a new resource group. The name of the resource and location refers to the rgname and location variables.

```
resource "azurerm_resource_group" "remotestaterg" {
  name     = var.rgname
  location = var.location
}
```

The code listing next provisions a new storage account in a resource group created in the previous step. The name is hard-coded here, but it can be easily changed to use a variable. The location and resource group name values are dependent on remotestaterg resource. The additional attributes account_tier and account_replication_type are required to provision a storage account (standard and GRS).

```
resource "azurerm_storage_account" "remotestatestorage" {
  name                     = "remotestatestorage"
  resource_group_name      = azurerm_resource_group.remotestaterg.name
```

```
location               = azurerm_resource_group.remotestaterg.location
account_tier           = "Standard"
account_replication_type = "GRS"

tags = {
  environment = "staging"
}
}
```

The next resource to provision is a container within the storage account. This storage account will store the Terraform state file. The name of the container is statefiles, and since state files should be stored securely, its access type is configured as private. This will ensure that storage account access keys or SAS tokens are required to access the content of the container.

```
resource "azurerm_storage_container" "remotestate-container" {
  name                  = "statefiles"
  storage_account_name  = azurerm_storage_account.remotestatestorage.name
  container_access_type = "private"
}
```

The next set of code listings will generate a token that can be used for accessing the content of the storage account. The first one will provide access to only the blob service. The token will be valid within the shown start and expiry dates. The content can be accessed only using the TLS protocol, and it would have read, write, delete, list, add, create, update and process permissions.

Data sources are another type of resource available within Terraform providers. Resources are meant to be provisioned, updated, or deleted. Data sources are different from these resources. They are meant for only reading the current state of resources. They help in providing the current state to other resources within the configuration.

```
data "azurerm_storage_account_sas" "storage-sas" {
  connection_string = azurerm_storage_account.remotestatestorage.primary_
  connection_string
  https_only        = true

  start  = "2020-12-25"
  expiry = "2021-10-20"
```

```
services {
  blob  = true
  queue = false
  table = false
  file  = false
}

  resource_types {
  service   = true
  container = true
  object    = true
}

 permissions {
  read    = true
  write   = true
  delete  = true
  list    = true
  add     = true
  create  = true
  update  = true
  process = true
 }

}
```

The next code listing can provide access only to a blob container within a storage account:

```
data "azurerm_storage_account_blob_container_sas" "container-sas" {
  connection_string = azurerm_storage_account.remotestatestorage.primary_
  connection_string
  container_name    = azurerm_storage_container.remotestate-container.name
  https_only        = true

  start  = "2020-12-25"
  expiry = "2021-10-20"
```

```
  permissions {
    read   = true
    add    = true
    create = true
    write  = true
    delete = true
    list   = true
  }

  cache_control           = "max-age=5"
  content_disposition = "inline"
  content_encoding    = "deflate"
  content_language    = "en-US"
  content_type        = "application/json"
}
```

Finally, to view and use the two SAS tokens, both of them are displayed after successful execution by Terraform using the output element.

```
output "sas_container_query_string" {
  value = data.azurerm_storage_account_blob_container_sas.container-sas.sas
}

output "sas_storage_query_string" {
  value = data.azurerm_storage_account_sas.storage-sas.sas
}
```

The script accepts a couple of variables, rgname and location, of type string, and they are defined using a simple variable element within the script.

```
variable rgname { type=  string}
variable location { type=  string}
```

There are multiple ways to supply values for variables declared within Terraform scripts. One of the ways is the use of the .tfvars file, and we will get into more details about them in the next section. We will create another file with the extension `.tfvars` within the same folder as the main Terraform script and add the following code into it:

```
rgname = "remotestoragerg"
location = "west europe"
```

Execute the previous script with the usual the Terraform CLI commands:

```
Terraform init
Terraform plan -var-file=variables.tfvars
Terraform apply -var-file=variables.tfvars
```

This will generate a SAS token similar to the following one:

```
sas_container_query_string = ?sv=2018-11-09&sr=c&st=2020-10-20&se=2021-10-
20&sp=racwdl&spr=https&rscc=max-age%3D5&rscd=inline&rsce=deflate&rscl=en-
US&rsct=application%2Fjson&sig=gh9GAWoFnZT5f64QkLj9HBOus0yKZKvv1rJ3ROMy6Kc%3D

sas_storage_query_string = ?sv=2017-07-29&ss=b&srt=sco&sp=rwdlacup&se=2021-
10-20&st=2020-10-21&spr=https&sig=L05MtT9ZiyTK%2Fp1Z%2FxMCLxuEa5jpLZkaGONMQ
iByUbA%3D
```

Now, that we have a storage account to store remote state, we can use it in other Terraform configurations and that is covered in next section.

Configurations Using Remote State

Now that we have the infrastructure for remote state provisioned and configured, it's time to create a Terraform script that will store its state in this remote storage.

Remote state is configured in Terraform scripts by configuring "backend". A *backend* is an umbrella term in Terraform and denotes a set of services that Terraform needs for its activities from a management perspective. Backends primarily consist of two important services.

- State management

- Workspace management

The following data is needed to configure the Azure storage account as a back end:

Resource_group_name: The name of resource group containing the storage account

storage_account_name: The name of the Azure storage account

container_name: The name of the blob container

key: The name of the state store file to be created

Sas_token: The security token needed to access a storage account

A sample script with remote storage configuration is shown next. The back-end configuration does not have sas_token listed as part of its configuration. This is because it is sensitive information and should not be hard-coded within files. It becomes difficult to change them, and also they introduce security risks and vulnerabilities. The value for this attribute should be supplied at runtime.

```
terraform {
    backend "azurerm" {
        resource_group_name   = "remotestoragerg"
        storage_account_name = "remotestatestorage"
        container_name        = "statefiles"
        key                   = "prod.terraform.tfstate"

    }
}

provider "azurerm" {
    version = "~>2.0"

    features {}
}

resource azurerm_resource_group rgname {
    name = "testrgforstate"
    location = "west europe"
}
```

```
output rgoutput {
    value = azurerm_resource_group.rgname
}
```

The SAS token needed to connect to the remote state can be supplied during the init command using the -backend-config option, as shown next:

terraform init -backend-config="sas_token=?sv=2018-11-09&sr=c&st=2020-12-25&se=2021-10-20&sp=racwdl&spr=https&rscc=max-age%3D5&rscd=inline&rsce=deflate&rscl=en-US&rsct=application%2Fjson&sig=5XpFqR2qgZjdw%2BQKfb%2BXs%2BKbUJTJwpXMiPXVfjzyOgw%3D"

After initialization, the rest of the commands such as plan and apply can be executed in a similar fashion as any other Terraform script.

Terraform will now know that it should not generate the state file in a local folder (the local folder is the default configuration in the Terraform backend) and instead will generate a state file named prod.terraform.tfstate in remote storage. This is shown in Figure 3-1.

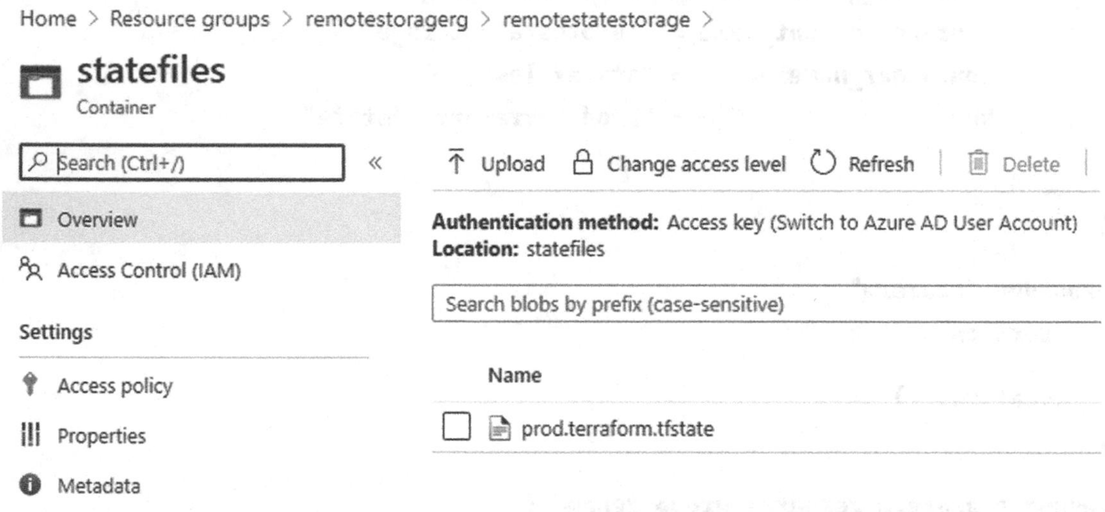

Home > Resource groups > remotestoragerg > remotestatestorage >

🗄 **statefiles**
Container

| 🔍 Search (Ctrl+/)   « | ↑ Upload   🔒 Change access level   ↻ Refresh   🗑 Delete |

🗖 Overview

🗝 Access Control (IAM)

Settings

📍 Access policy

▥ Properties

ⓘ Metadata

Authentication method: Access key (Switch to Azure AD User Account)
Location: statefiles

Search blobs by prefix (case-sensitive)

Name

☐ 📄 prod.terraform.tfstate

Figure 3-1. *Azure storage container storing remote Terraform state file*

Terraform Files

All the code for Terraform scripts can be authored in a single name having the extension ".tf". Terraform will load, parse, and interpret the file reading the blocks and then executing them logically. The order of execution of blocks in Terraform script is:

- terraform

- provider

- variable

- locals

- resource

- module

- output

As mentioned before, all of these blocks can be authored within a single file; however, each of these can also be authored in their own file with each having a .tf extension. Terraform will assemble all these files together before executing them as a single script. The folder becomes a unit for the script execution, and all files within a folder are combined to work as a single Terraform unit and script.

Breaking down a large monolith Terraform file into smaller manageable file is far better and ideal file structure compared to a single file. The script becomes much more comprehendible, easier to read and helps in faster code editing.

To understand this better, let's create a new folder named TerraformFileStructure and further create multiple .tf files in it, each one responsible for declaring different blocks of code.

The goal of these files together is a create a resource group on Azure based on values from variables for resource group name and locations.

- Variables.tf: This file contains the variables declaration.

- Versions.tf: This file contains the terraform configuration related to provider and Terraform versioning.

- Providers.tf: This file contains the provider configuration.

- `Locals.tf`: This file contains the definitions of `local` variables.

- `main.tf`: This file contains resource and module configurations. This file can further be broken into multiple files, each containing different sets of resources. We will look into this pattern later in the next chapter.

- `Output.tf`: This file contains the output blocks.

Code for variables.tf

The `variables.tf` file contains just the variable declaration. Three variables, called `rgname`, `location`, and `environment` of type `string` are declared in this file.

```
variable rgname {
    type = string
}
variable location {
    type = string
}
variable environment {
    type = string
}
```

Code for versions.tf

This file contains the `terraform` configuration related to provider and their version numbers. The `terraform` configuration helps to define the dependency on the Terraform CLI version using the `required_version` setting. In the code listing shown next, the Terraform CLI version is 0.13.3. The Terraform configuration also helps in configuring the provider plugins used within the scripts using their source name and version numbers. The `azurerm` provider plugin is declared within `required_providers` with multiple version conditions.

```
terraform {
    required_version = "0.13.3"
    required_providers {
        azurerm = {
            source  = "registry.terraform.io/hashicorp/azurerm"
            version = "~>2.36, ~>2.40"

        }
    }
}
```

Code for providers.tf

The providers.tf file contains the configuration for the provider itself. This could include the authentication information for connecting to the target cloud platform. In this case, it just contains the mandatory empty features {} element(for now, it will be expanded in subsequent chapters).

```
provider azurerm {
    features {}
}
```

Code for locals.tf

The locals file contains the locals block and generates local variables using values from variables supplied during execution. The code listing next uses the variables rgname and environment by concatenating them into a single resourcegroupname variable.

```
locals {
    resourcegroupname = "${var.rgname}-${var.environment}"
}
```

Code for main.tf

This file contains the resources to be created. For this example, it contains a single resource_group definition and uses both a local as well as global variable for its attributes.

```
resource azurerm_resource_group rg {
    name= local.resourcegroupname
    location = var.location
}
```

Code for outputs.tf

The script execution will also contain a single output: the identifier of resource group. This is a runtime dynamically generated identifier and is returned by the script as output. The code listing shown next uses the resource group name along with its "id" property. The id is then assigned to the value attribute of the output block.

```
output resourcegroupid {
    value = azurerm_resource_group.rg.id
}
```

Code for values.tfvars

Finally, there is a values.tfvars file that contains all the values for the global variables. Since values for three global variables are expected, all the three values are provided in this file.

```
rgname = "filestructureexample"
location = "west europe"
environment = "dev"
```

Executing the Terraform script will result in the creation of a resource group. The Terraform commands are shown next. It is to be noted that there are multiple ways to provide values for global variables, and .tfvars is just one of them. We will explore other ways in the next chapter. The values for variables must be supplied while executing both the plan and apply commands.

```
terraform init
```

```
terraform plan -var-file=values.tfvar
```

```
terraform apply -var-file=values.tfvar -auto-approve
```

The result after successful execution of apply command is shown next.

Apply complete! Resources: 1 added, 0 changed, 0 destroyed.

Outputs:
resourcegroupid = /subscriptions/9755ffce-e94b-4332-9be8-1ade15e78909/
resourceGroups/filestructureexample-dev

Summary

This chapter focused on some of the elementary but important concepts related
to Terraform. Terraform scripts are heavily dependent on the local, output, and
global variables. It is important to understand how to use these variables. There
are multiple data types: simple, collection and structural types available in Terraform.
The chapter detailed the usage of all the types of variables available within Terraform.
This chapter also covered provider plugins along with versioning. Storing Terraform
state in remote storage is the crux for successfully using Terraform within a team, and
a complete walk-through of using an Azure storage account as remote storage was
also covered. Finally, file layouts become quite important, especially in large projects
for better manageability and readability. Breaking the Terraform script into multiple
logical and physical files is an important skill for Terraform developers and this was also
covered using an example. The next chapter will focus on the programmability aspects of
Terraform.

CHAPTER 4

Deep-Dive into Terraform

Terraform provides a declarative based language through which the desired state of the resources is configured. The configuration comprises of name-value pairs; the name refers to specific configuration elements exposed by the resource, and the value is the desired configuration Terraform does not provide a full blown scripting language and so it is not possible to write imperative scripts that are usually possible in a general scripting language like Bash or PowerShell.

However, Terraform provides few constructs that we can use to implement some nuances related to programming like looping and conditional statements. In this chapter, we will explore some of these constructs provided by Terraform to help write dynamic configurations instead of copy pasting blocks of same code repeatedly.

These programming constructs help in writing smaller, manageable configurations that are easy to read and change.

Base Configuration

We will use the next shown Terraform configuration as the base configuration to explore its programming aspects. We will keep modifying it throughout this chapter. The configuration requires version 0.14 of the `terraform` and version 2.53.0 of the `azurerm` provider. It accepts three parameters: `resource_group_name` for the name of the resource group, `resource_group_location` for the location of the resources and resource group, and `storage_account_name` for the name of the storage account. The configuration provisions two resources: an Azure resource group and a storage account. The last configuration block outputs the storage account's unique identifier as part of the execution.

© Ritesh Modi 2021
R. Modi, *Deep-Dive Terraform on Azure*, https://doi.org/10.1007/978-1-4842-7328-9_4

```
terraform {
  required_providers {
    azurerm = {
      source  = "hashicorp/azurerm"
      version = "=2.53.0"
    }
  }

  required_version = "~> 0.14"
}

provider "azurerm" {
  features {}
}

variable resource_group_name { type= string }
variable resource_group_location { type= string }
variable storage_account_name { type= string }

resource "azurerm_resource_group" "resource_group" {
  name     = var.resource_group_name
  location = var.resource_group_location
}

resource "azurerm_storage_account" "storage_account" {
  name = var.storage_account_name
  location                = azurerm_resource_group.resource_group.location
  resource_group_name = azurerm_resource_group.resource_group.name
  account_replication_type = "LRS"
  account_tier            = "Standard"
  account_kind            = "StorageV2"
  min_tls_version         = "TLS1_2"

  enable_https_traffic_only = true
}

output storage_account_ids {
    value = azurerm_storage_account.storage_account.id
}
```

This configuration can be executed using the `terraform apply` command as shown next. The values for the three variables are supplied as part of the command-line execution.

It is important to authenticate using the `az login` command prior to executing Terraform commands. Terraform uses the logged in user to authenticate to Azure.

```
Terraform init
```

```
terraform apply -var="resource_group_name=simpletfexample" -var="resource_
group_location=westeurope" -var="storage_account_name=simpletfstorage"
```

The result of the execution is the provisioning of the resource group and storage account on Azure, as shown in Figure 4-1. The output `"storage_account_ids"` contains the unique identifier of the storage account.

```
azurerm_resource_group.resource_group: Creating...
azurerm_resource_group.resource_group: Creation complete after 2s [id=/subscriptions/9755ffce-e94b-4332-9be8-1ade15e78909/resourceGroups/simpletfexample]
azurerm_storage_account.storage_account: Creating...
azurerm_storage_account.storage_account: Still creating... [10s elapsed]
azurerm_storage_account.storage_account: Still creating... [20s elapsed]
azurerm_storage_account.storage_account: Still creating... [30s elapsed]
azurerm_storage_account.storage_account: Creation complete after 34s [id=/subscriptions/9755ffce-e94b-4332-9be8-1ade15e78909/resourceGroups/simpletfexample/providers/Microsoft.Storage/st
orageAccounts/simpletfstorage]

Apply complete! Resources: 2 added, 0 changed, 0 destroyed.

Outputs:

storage_account_ids = [
  "/subscriptions/9755ffce-e94b-4332-9be8-1ade15e78909/resourceGroups/simpletfexample/providers/Microsoft.Storage/storageAccounts/simpletfstorage",
]
```

Figure 4-1. *Terraform execution output*

Now that we understand the base configuration, we will use it to explore the programmability aspects of Terraform.

count

A frequent requirement while working with Azure and other cloud services is to provision resources such as storage accounts with multiple instances. The majority configuration for each instance remain the same, however, they might differ in some of the properties like the name property. Still, the structure and configuration settings are similar to other instances. One way to solve such a problem is to repeatedly declare resource blocks and modify only those properties that make them distinct instances. This solution has some major drawbacks, especially around maintainability and upgradability. Any change would have to replicated across all such resources and increases the overall chances for error in spite of considerable testing. The configuration files can also become quite large and nonreadable.

Terraform provides the count meta-element that helps in solving this problem in an elegant manner. Count helps in implementing a loop just like a for loop in other programming languages. The count attribute can be added to any resource, and the value of this attribute determines the number of resource instances to be provisioned. The count of instances starts from zero, and the provisioning of the resource instance continues until it matches the number specified for the count attribute. For example, a value of 3 for the count property for a resource configuration will provision four resources starting from 0 all the way up until the count reaches 3.

count has an index property that provides its current value during iterations. This is the current value while the iteration is in progress, and it increments by one for every iteration. This property is quite useful as it can be used to name the resources uniquely and can also be used to index array's to assign dynamic values to properties. For example, storage account names in Azure should be uniquely named and by appending the index value to the name of the storage account in every iteration, the storage account can be named uniquely. There are other ways to provide different values to resource properties using the count.index property, which will be covered in the next section.

The code listing shown next has a few changes highlighted in bold. There is the addition of the count meta-element in the azurerm_storage_account resource, and the name of its resource group is not directly dependent on a variable anymore.

The configuration accepts an additional variable called nos_of_storage_accounts. This value determines the number of storage accounts to be created. The count attribute gets its value from this variable. The storage account name should be unique, and another concept known as *string templates* or *string interpolation* is used to make it unique. This concept will be covered later in this chapter. ${var.storage_account_name}${count.index} uses string interpolation to concatenate the storage account name with the current index and assign it as the name of the storage account.

```
terraform {
  required_providers {
    azurerm = {
      source  = "hashicorp/azurerm"
      version = "=2.53.0"
    }
  }

  required_version = "~> 0.14"
}
```

```
provider "azurerm" {
  features {}
}

variable resource_group_name { type=string }
variable resource_group_location { type=string }
variable storage_account_name { type=string }
variable nos_of_storage_accounts { type=number }

resource "azurerm_resource_group" "resource_group" {
  name     = var.resource_group_name
  location = var.resource_group_location
}

resource "azurerm_storage_account" "storage_account" {
  count = var.nos_of_storage_accounts
  name = "${var.storage_account_name}${count.index}"
  location                = azurerm_resource_group.resource_group.location
  resource_group_name = azurerm_resource_group.resource_group.name
  account_replication_type = "LRS"
  account_tier            = "Standard"
  account_kind            = "StorageV2"
  min_tls_version         = "TLS1_2"

  enable_https_traffic_only = true
}

output storage_account_ids {
    value = azurerm_storage_account.storage_account[*].id
}
```

Splatting

It is important to understand that there is a single block and resource declaration with a single Terraform identifier called storage_account. However, Terraform produces multiple resources, and there should be a way to refer to those resources by name. Terraform generates names for each resource under the count iteration. Terraform generates an array of resources, and each resource can be accessed using an array indexer. For example, the first `storage_account` can be accessed using the `storage_account[0]` identifier, and subsequent ones can be accessed using incremental index values. Once the resources are provisioned using the `count` property, they are stored and named in a Terraform state as an array.

It can become challenging to refer to these resources that have dynamically generated names. Either the names should be hard-coded (notice the array index 0) like `azurerm_storage_account.storage_account[0].id` or there should be a better way to address and refer them together.

Terraform provides the splatting (*) operator that can be used to access all values within a list or array. All the elements of the list will be returned as a result of using it. For example, `azurerm_storage_account.storage_account[*]` will output all the complete storage accounts details provisioned as part of the `count` iterations. Similarly, the `azurerm_storage_account.storage_account[*].id` will return all the storage account identifiers for all storage accounts provisioned as part of count loop.

The output from the previous listing outputs all the storage account identifiers using the splat operator, as shown in Figure 4-2.

```
Apply complete! Resources: 3 added, 0 changed, 1 destroyed.

Outputs:

storage_account_ids = [
  "/subscriptions/9755ffce-e94b-4332-9be8-1ade15e78909/resourceGroups/simpletfexample/providers/Microsoft.Storage/storageAccounts/simpletfstorage0",
  "/subscriptions/9755ffce-e94b-4332-9be8-1ade15e78909/resourceGroups/simpletfexample/providers/Microsoft.Storage/storageAccounts/simpletfstorage1",
  "/subscriptions/9755ffce-e94b-4332-9be8-1ade15e78909/resourceGroups/simpletfexample/providers/Microsoft.Storage/storageAccounts/simpletfstorage2",
]
```

Figure 4-2. *Terraform execution output for count meta-attribute*

The previously listed configuration can be executed using Terraform as shown next. It has an additional parameter, `nos_of_storage_accounts`, with a value of 3. This means the configuration should provision three storage accounts with distinct names based on the index values.

```
terraform apply -var="resource_group_name=simpletfexample" -var="resource_group_location=westeurope" -var="storage_account_name=simpletfstorage" -var="nos_of_storage_accounts=3"
```

terraform destroy

So far, all the concepts and examples have related to applying the Terraform configuration to provision new resources or reconfigure them. However, there are times we will want to remove or delete resources. Terraform provides the destroy command that can remove resources from the actual environment and also from the state file so that Terraform does not track these resources anymore. The next command shows the usage of destroy command. It would require the same value for variables and command options as used during the terraform apply command. It will remove the resources both from the state file as well as from actual environment.

```
terraform destroy  -var="resource_group_name=simpletfexample"
-var="resource_group_location=westeurope" -var="storage_account_
name=simpletfstorage" -var="nos_of_storage_accounts=3"
```

The destroy command is actually an alias to the terraform apply -destroy command, which can be used in place of the terraform destroy command.

Sometimes a subset of resources may need to be removed. Individual resources can be targeted and removed using the destroy command along with the target resource details, as shown in the next command listing. Notice the target option has a value of azurerm_storage_account.storage_account[1]. This is the storage account name stored in the state file as second item in array generated by the Count meta-argument. It will just remove a single storage account referred to from the state file as azurerm_storage_account.storage_account[1].

```
terraform destroy -target azurerm_storage_account.storage_account[1]
-var="resource_group_name=simpletfexample" -var="resource_group_
location=westeurope" -var="storage_account_name=simpletfstorage" -var="nos_
of_storage_accounts=3"
```

Figure 4-3 shows the result of removing a storage account using the terraform destroy command. Multiple target options can be used simultaneously to refer to multiple resources for removal.

```
Warning: Applied changes may be incomplete

The plan was created with the -target option in effect, so some changes requested in the configuration may have been ignored and the output values may not be fully updated. Run the
following command to verify that no other changes are pending:
    terraform plan

Note that the -target option is not suitable for routine use, and is provided only for exceptional situations such as recovering from errors or mistakes, or when Terraform
specifically suggests to use it as part of an error message.

Destroy complete! Resources: 1 destroyed.
```

Figure 4-3. *Terraform execution output for the destroy command*

count with List Variables

The previous section showed how to use count and its index property to uniquely name the storage account using string interpolation. However, storage account names can be supplied as a list of values through variables. This way a list of storage account names can be used to name each storage account. Terraform provides the length function, and it provides the count of items in a list as an output. The value from the length function can be assigned to the count property. This will ensure that the count will iterate as many numbers of times as the number of items in the provided list.

It is also important to understand the mechanism used to assign the values from the list to the name property of the storage account. This is done by indexing the list variable and passing the index obtained using the count.index property.

```
terraform {
  required_providers {
    azurerm = {
      source  = "hashicorp/azurerm"
      version = "=2.53.0"
    }
  }

  required_version = "~> 0.14"
}

provider "azurerm" {
  features {}
}

variable resource_group_name { type=string }
variable resource_group_location { type=string }
variable storage_account_names { type=list }

resource "azurerm_resource_group" "resource_group" {
  name     = var.resource_group_name
  location = var.resource_group_location
}
```

```
resource "azurerm_storage_account" "storage_account" {
  count = length(var.storage_account_names)
  name = "${var.storage_account_names[count.index]}"
  location              = azurerm_resource_group.resource_group.location
  resource_group_name = azurerm_resource_group.resource_group.name
  account_replication_type = "LRS"
  account_tier           = "Standard"
  account_kind           = "StorageV2"
  min_tls_version        = "TLS1_2"

  enable_https_traffic_only = true
}

output storage_account_ids {
  value = azurerm_storage_account.storage_account[*].id
}
```

Applying the configuration needs three variable values this time and is shown here. Notice that a list with two storage account names is passed as value to the variable storage_account_names.

```
terraform apply -var="resource_group_name=simpletfexample" -var="resource_
group_location=westeurope" -var='storage_account_names=["tfliststorage1",
"tfliststorage2"]'
```

Figure 4-4 shows the output from the terraform apply execution.

```
Apply complete! Resources: 2 added, 0 changed, 3 destroyed.
Outputs:
storage_account_ids = [
  "/subscriptions/9755ffce-e94b-4332-9be8-1ade15e78909/resourceGroups/simpletfexample/providers/Microsoft.Storage/storageAccounts/tfliststorage1",
  "/subscriptions/9755ffce-e94b-4332-9be8-1ade15e78909/resourceGroups/simpletfexample/providers/Microsoft.Storage/storageAccounts/tfliststorage2",
]
```

Figure 4-4. *Terraform execution output from using the count meta-argument with a list containing storage account name*

Conditional Statements

Configurations in Terraform are executed based on the dependency graph between the resources. All resources without any dependencies are provisioned in parallel, and then the dependent resources are provisioned. However, there are times when resources need to be created only if a condition or set of conditions is true or false.

Terraform does not offer any construct that provides features related to the conditional provisioning of resources. There are means to get around this limitation using the count meta-element.

It is better to explain the concept of conditional provisioning of resources using an example. Let's say we want to provision a storage account in "east us" if the value is true for storage_account_eastus variable. If the value is false, we would like to provision the storage account in "west us". This can easily be implemented using two resource definitions, as shown here. The first storage account has a count meta-element set to a condition. If the condition is true, it returns 1; otherwise, it returns 0. It means that if the value of the storage_account_eastus variable is true, the count property for storage_account_eastus resources gets the value 1 and a storage account is provisioned in the "east us" region.

```
resource "azurerm_storage_account" "storage_account_eastus" {
  count = var.storage_account_eastus ==  true ? 1 : 0
  name = var.storage_account_name
  location            = "eastus"
  resource_group_name = azurerm_resource_group.resource_group.name
  account_replication_type = "LRS"
  account_tier            = "Standard"
  account_kind            = "StorageV2"
  min_tls_version         = "TLS1_2"

  enable_https_traffic_only = true
}
```

On the other hand, there is another definition of a storage account in the same configuration, as shown next. The name of the Terraform resource is storage_account_westus, and it will provision the storage account in "west us" only if the value for storage_account_eastus is false. Combining the configuration for this and prior storage account, it is evident that any one storage account would be provisioned depending on the value of variable storage_account_eastus. is either true or false.

```
resource "azurerm_storage_account" "storage_account_westus" {
  count = var.storage_account_eastus == false ? 1 : 0
  name = var.storage_account_name
  location               = "westus"
  resource_group_name = azurerm_resource_group.resource_group.name
  account_replication_type = "LRS"
  account_tier           = "Standard"
  account_kind           = "StorageV2"
  min_tls_version        = "TLS1_2"

  enable_https_traffic_only = true
}
```

The complete code listing for the conditional provisioning of the storage account is shown next:

```
terraform {
  required_providers {
    azurerm = {
      source  = "hashicorp/azurerm"
      version = "=2.53.0"
    }
  }

  required_version = "~> 0.14"
}

provider "azurerm" {
  features {}
}

variable resource_group_name { type=string }
variable resource_group_location { type=string }
variable storage_account_name { type=string }
variable storage_account_eastus { type=bool }
```

```
resource "azurerm_resource_group" "resource_group" {
  name     = var.resource_group_name
  location = var.resource_group_location
}

resource "azurerm_storage_account" "storage_account_eastus" {
  count = var.storage_account_eastus ==   true ? 1 : 0
  name = var.storage_account_name
  location             = "eastus"
  resource_group_name = azurerm_resource_group.resource_group.name
  account_replication_type = "LRS"
  account_tier             = "Standard"
  account_kind             = "StorageV2"
  min_tls_version          = "TLS1_2"

  enable_https_traffic_only = true
}

resource "azurerm_storage_account" "storage_account_westus" {
  count = var.storage_account_eastus == false ? 1 : 0
  name = var.storage_account_name
  location             = "westus"
  resource_group_name = azurerm_resource_group.resource_group.name
  account_replication_type = "LRS"
  account_tier             = "Standard"
  account_kind             = "StorageV2"
  min_tls_version          = "TLS1_2"

  enable_https_traffic_only = true
}

output storage_account_id_westus {
    value = azurerm_storage_account.storage_account_westus[*].id
}

output storage_account_location_westus {
    value = azurerm_storage_account.storage_account_westus[*].location
}
```

```
output storage_account_id_eastus {
    value = azurerm_storage_account.storage_account_eastus[*].id
}

output storage_account_location_eastus {
    value = azurerm_storage_account.storage_account_eastus[*].location
}
```

The Terraform command to apply the configuration is shown next:

```
terraform apply -var="resource_group_name=simpletfexample" -var="resource_group_location=westeurope" -var='storage_account_name=conditionaltfstorage' -var=storage_account_eastus=false
```

The result from the execution is that the storage account is provisioned at "west US" because the value for storage_account_eastus is false, as shown in Figure 4-5.

```
Apply complete! Resources: 1 added, 0 changed, 1 destroyed.

Outputs:

storage_account_id_eastus = []
storage_account_id_westus = [
  "/subscriptions/9755ffce-e94b-4332-9be8-1ade15e78909/resourceGroups/simpletfexample/providers/Microsoft.Storage/storageAccounts/conditionaltfstorage",
]
storage_account_location_eastus = []
storage_account_location_westus = [
  "westus",
]
```

Figure 4-5. *Terraform execution output for conditional resources*

If the value of storage_account_eastus is set to true as in the next shown command, the storage account would be provisioned at "east US", as shown in Figure 4-6.

```
terraform apply -var="resource_group_name=simpletfexample" -var="resource_group_location=westeurope" -var='storage_account_name=conditionaltfstorage' -var=storage_account_eastus=true
```

```
Apply complete! Resources: 1 added, 0 changed, 1 destroyed.

Outputs:

storage_account_id_eastus = [
  "/subscriptions/9755ffce-e94b-4332-9be8-1ade15e78909/resourceGroups/simpletfexample/providers/Microsoft.Storage/storageAccounts/conditionaltfstorage",
]
storage_account_id_westus = []
storage_account_location_eastus = [
  "eastus",
]
storage_account_location_westus = []
```

Figure 4-6. *Terraform execution output for conditional resources*

for_each

Terraform provides another meta-element, for_each, which is more versatile and feature rich compared to count for looping and creating multiple resource instances. for_each works with both Terraform sets and maps. for_each not only helps in looping at the resource level (similar to count) but also loops at the resource property level. Let's look at the usage of for_each for both at the instance and property levels.

for_each provides two meta-elements: each.key and each.value. These are useful in retrieving individual key and values from a map during iterations.

For example, a sample map shown here can be iterated using for_each meta-element:

```
{
    "rgcommon" : "west US",
     "rgnetworking" : "east US",
     "rgappservices" : "east US"
}
```

While iterating the previous map with for_each, for each iteration, the each.key meta-element will contain rgcommon, rgnetworking, and rgappservices as its value During the same iteration, each.value meta-element will contain west US, east US, and east US values respectively.

The next code listing provisions storage accounts using the for_each looping construct. There is just a single storage account resource definition, and it accepts a map consisting of name-value pairs. The name will refer to the name of the storage account, and the value will refer to the region of the storage account.

The variable storage_account_info of type map is used along with the for_each attribute. The map value is assigned to for_each meta-element as part of resource declaration. The name attribute of storage accounts gets its value from the each.key property, and the location attribute gets its value from each.value. This is shown in bold in the next code listing:

```
terraform {
  required_providers {
    azurerm = {
      source  = "hashicorp/azurerm"
      version = "=2.53.0"
    }
```

```
  }
}

provider "azurerm" {
  features {}
}

variable resource_group_name { type=string }
variable resource_group_location { type=string }
variable storage_account_info { type=map }

resource "azurerm_resource_group" "resource_group" {
  name     = var.resource_group_name
  location = var.resource_group_location
}

resource "azurerm_storage_account" "storage_account" {
  for_each = var.storage_account_info
  name = each.key
  location                  = each.value
  resource_group_name = azurerm_resource_group.resource_group.name
  account_replication_type = "LRS"
  account_tier             = "Standard"
  account_kind             = "StorageV2"
  min_tls_version          = "TLS1_2"

  enable_https_traffic_only = true
}

output storage_account_location_eastus {
    value = azurerm_storage_account.storage_account["mapstoragename1"].name
}
```

The value for the map should be provided while executing the Terraform configuration. The variables can be filled in multiple ways, and providing them using a command line is shown next. The variable storage_account_info is provided with a JSON string consisting of name-value pairs, each representing a combination of storage account name and its corresponding Azure region.

```
terraform apply -var="resource_group_name=simpletfexample"
-var="resource_group_location=westeurope" -var='storage_account_info={
"mapstoragename1":"westus", "mapstoragename2": "eastus"  }'
```

The configuration has a single output that outputs the name of the storage account by looking up the resource map by its name. Figure 4-7 shows the output.

```
Apply complete! Resources: 0 added, 0 changed, 0 destroyed.

Outputs:

storage_account_location_eastus = "mapstoragename1"
```

Figure 4-7. *Terraform execution output using for-each meta-argument*

Difference Between for_each and count

After going through the previous two sections of this chapter, you might be wondering what exactly the differences between count and for_each are. They are similar in their implementation; both are able to loop through a collection and provide current values in each iteration. Although both for_each and count look similar, they are quite different in their usage. One of the primary differences between for_each and count is that for_each generates a map of resource instances, while count generates an array of resources. We can access a map using its key and it does not have indexer. This means a numerical value cannot be used to get the resource at that position. A key of type string can be used to access the resource instance.

for_each at the Property Level

for_each not only helps in resource iteration but is also capable of property iteration. for_each accepts set, map, and list collection types for property iteration. There are some resources that can have multiple property instances. For example, Azure App Services can have multiple connection string settings. A connection string entity for an app service comprises of three values - a name, type, and value. Property iterations use "dynamic" keyword along with the name of the property. Within the dynamic block, for_each is defined with a content block. The content block is iterated for each item in the collection assigned to for_each and the collection values then become available within the content block. The values in collection are available using the dynamic property qualifier within the content block. The usage of dynamic property iteration is shown next:

```
dynamic "connection_string" {
  for_each = var.connection_strings
  content {
    name  = connection_string.name
    type  = connection_string.type
    value = connection_string.value
  }
}
```

The next code listing provisions a resource group, an app service plan, and an app service. The app service has a dynamic connection_string element through which we can iterate and generate multiple instance for a property. After the iterations are complete, the app service will have multiple connection strings defined, one for each item in the collection.

```
terraform {
  required_providers {
    azurerm = {
      source  = "hashicorp/azurerm"
      version = "=2.53.0"
    }
  }

  required_version = "~> 0.14"
}

provider "azurerm" {
  features {}
}

variable resource_group_name { type=string }
variable resource_group_location { type=string }
variable custom_tags { type=map }
variable app_service_plan_name { type=string }
```

```
variable app_service_plan_kind{ type=string }
variable app_service_plan_sku { type = map }
variable app_service_name{ type=string }
variable connection_strings { type = list(object(
    {
        name = string,
        type = string,
        value = string
    }
)))}

locals {
    default_tags = {
        "department" : "finance",
        "owner" : "riteshmodi"
    }

    app_size = "B2"
}

resource "azurerm_resource_group" "resource_group" {
  name      = var.resource_group_name
  location = var.resource_group_location
}

resource "azurerm_app_service_plan" "app_service_plan" {
  name = var.app_service_plan_name

  location             = azurerm_resource_group.resource_group.location
  resource_group_name = azurerm_resource_group.resource_group.name
  kind                 = var.app_service_plan_kind
  reserved             = var.app_service_plan_kind == "Linux" ? true : false

  sku {
    capacity = lookup(var.app_service_plan_sku, "capacity", null)
    size     = lookup(var.app_service_plan_sku, "size", null)
    tier     = lookup(var.app_service_plan_sku, "tier", null)
  }
```

```
  tags = merge(local.default_tags, var.custom_tags)
}

resource "azurerm_app_service" "app_service" {
  name                  = var.app_service_name
  location              = azurerm_resource_group.resource_group.location
  resource_group_name   = azurerm_resource_group.resource_group.name
  app_service_plan_id   = azurerm_app_service_plan.app_service_plan.id

  dynamic "connection_string" {
    for_each = var.connection_strings
    content {
      name  = lookup(connection_string.value, "name", null)
      type  = lookup(connection_string.value, "type", null)
      value = lookup(connection_string.value, "value", null)
    }
  }

  https_only              = true
}

output app_service_plan_identifier {
    value = azurerm_app_service_plan.app_service_plan.id
}
```

The terraform apply command is similar to previous commands used for other Terraform configurations. The connection_strings variable is of type list(object). This means it will accept multiple objects each consisting of three attributes: name, type, and value. For each object, a new connection string property will be generated using the for_each iteration.

```
terraform apply -var="resource_group_name=simpletfexampleforeach"
-var="resource_group_location=westeurope" -var='custom_tags={
"environment":"dev", "projectname": "terraformbook"  }' -var='app_
service_plan_name=tfbookappplan' -var='app_service_plan_kind=Linux'
-var='app_service_plan_sku={ "capacity": 2, "size": "B2", "tier":"Basic" }'
-var='connection_strings=[{"name":"EmployeeConnection","type":"SQLSERVER","
value":"sqlserverconnectioninfo"}]' -var='app_service_name=tfbookwebapp'
```

Figure 4-8 shows the end result due to execution of the prior configuration. It creates a connection string with `employeeconnection` as its name, SQL Server as the type, and the connection string value as its value. These values are passed using the command line using the `connection_strings` variable.

Connection strings

Connection strings are encrypted at rest and transmitted over an encrypted channel.

+ New connection string   👁 Show values   ✐ Advanced edit

| Filter connection strings |

Name	Value	Source	Type	Deployme...	Delete	Edit
EmployeeConnection	👁 Hidden value. Click to	App Service Config	SQLServer		🗑	✐

Figure 4-8. *Connection string app settings in Azure App Services*

for Expressions (Input Map – Output Map)

Terraform also supports `"for"` expressions. The `count` attribute inherently provides a `for` loop that starts from 0 and iterates until it reaches to the end of the collection. `for_each` does not take the count and length into consideration; rather, it keeps iterating through each item in collection and stops once all the items have been visited.

`for` expressions are not meant for resource or resource-property iterations. They provide more fine-grained control over the collection iteration.

`for` expressions can iterate over any collection type in Terraform. It can iterate over a map, set, or list. If it iterates over a map, it provides access to both the key and the value portion of the map. Similarly, if it iterates over a set or a list, it provides access to each value stored within the set or the list.

The output returned from a `for` expression is a collection, and it could be a map or a list.

Let's see some examples of a `for` expression.

```
{for name, location in var.storage_account_info: lower(name) =>
upper(location)}
```

In the prior example, the `for` expression iterates over a map as specified in the first segment of the expression.

```
for name, location in var.storage_account_info
```

The for expression generates a key-value pair for each item in the map. While generating the new map, it converts the key into lowercase and the value into uppercase. The return values

```
lower(name) => upper(location)
```

is enclosed within opening and closing brackets denoting that the output is of type Map. The => is a special operator that is used in Terraform to generate key-value pairs.

Let's see another example of a for expression that outputs a list after iterating through a Map collection.

```
[for name, location in var.storage_account_info: "${name}-${location}"]
```

In this example, the for expression iterates over a map, but this time it generates a single value for each item in the Map collection. The single item comprises of values derived from both the key and value in the Map collection. All the values generated are returned as a List collection. The return values

```
"${name}-${location}"
```

are enclosed within opening and closing brackets denoting that the output is of type List.

Now, it's time to apply the already gained knowledge on for expressions within the Terraform configuration. The output from the configuration is derived using the for loop, iterating over the storage_account_info variable, which is a collection of type Map.

```
terraform {
  required_providers {
    azurerm = {
      source  = "hashicorp/azurerm"
      version = "=2.53.0"
    }
  }

  required_version = "~> 0.14"
}
```

```
provider "azurerm" {
  features {}
}

variable storage_account_info { type=map }

output storage_account_location_eastus {
    value = {for name, location in var.storage_account_info: lower(name) =>
upper(location)}
}
```

The configuration is applied using the command line, as shown next. It is important to note the value for the variable storage_account_info. It is a collection consisting of two items: the name of the resource group and its related Azure region.

```
terraform apply -var='storage_account_info={ "mapstoragename1":"westus",
"mapstoragename2": "eastus"  }'
```

The output is a map consisting of keys and values from the for loop, as shown in Figure 4-9.

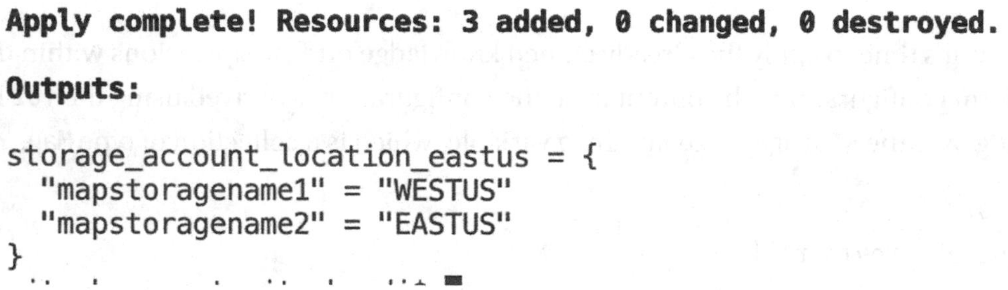

```
Apply complete! Resources: 3 added, 0 changed, 0 destroyed.

Outputs:

storage_account_location_eastus = {
    "mapstoragename1" = "WESTUS"
    "mapstoragename2" = "EASTUS"
}
```

Figure 4-9. *Terraform execution output using for expression*

for Expressions (Input Map – Output List)

As discussed in the previous section, it is possible to accept a Map collection for iteration and generate a List collection as output. If we replace the output block in the previous code listing with the output block mentioned next, the terraform apply command would generate the output consisting of the resource group name in lowercase in a List collection.

```
output storage_account_location_eastus {
    value = [for name, location in var.storage_account_info: lower(name)]
}
```

You will notice that the output from executing the this Terraform configuration consists of a List collection consisting of the resource group names, all in lowercase, as shown in Figure 4-10.

Apply complete! Resources: 0 added, 0 changed, 0 destroyed.

Outputs:

```
storage_account_location_eastus = [
    "mapstoragename1",
    "mapstoragename2",
]
```

Figure 4-10. *Terraform execution output with for expression (map input and list output)*

It is also possible to interpolate the key-value pairs in a meaningful way and generate an output List collection, as shown here:

```
output storage_account_location_eastus {
    value = [for name, location in var.storage_account_info: "${name}-
    ${location}"]
}
```

Figure 4-11 shows the output from using the previous block.

Apply complete! Resources: 0 added, 0 changed, 0 destroyed.

Outputs:

```
storage_account_location_eastus = [
    "mapstoragename1-westus",
    "mapstoragename2-eastus",
]
```

Figure 4-11. *Terraform execution output with FOR expression (map input and list output)*

String Templating

Terraform provides rich capabilities with regard to string manipulation. Generally, strings require manipulation including combining static values with references to variables, using resources, and mutating strings using functions. Terraform provides two template-based solutions for generating strings based on dynamic values.

String Interpolation

String interpolation refers to expressions that are evaluated at runtime and returns dynamic string value by manipulating existing values in a meaningful way. This string could be combination of multiple string values and those could come from string variables, resource properties returning string value or just static string literal value. When Terraform encounters an expression containing string interpolation, it evaluates the expression, resolves the references, generates and returns a new string in lieu of the expression. The string interpolation expression is always within double-quotes, and the references to variables or other resources are enclosed within ${} syntax.

An example of string interpolation with all subexpressions being variables is here:

```
"${var.stack}-${var.client_name}-${var.environment}"
```

The return value after the evaluation of this expression would be hyphen-separated values composed using stack, client_name, and the environment variable.

An example of string interpolation with a combination of a static string literal and variables is shown here:

```
"${var.stack}-${var.client_name}-dev"
```

The return value after the evaluation of this expression would be hyphen-separated values stored in stack, the client_name variable, and the dev literal string.

String Directives

Terraform provides another string template-based solution, and it is a more advanced implementation compared to string interpolation. One of the limitations of string interpolation is that it does not allow conditional statements and looping within the expressions. String directives help to overcome this limitation. String directives allow developers to implement conditional statements and loop within strings. The string could be a here-doc or a single-line string.

The string directives are defined using the %{} syntax. Within the brackets, it is possible to define conditional statements and loops.

It is much easier to explain and understand string directives using a simple Terraform configuration, as shown here:

```
terraform {
  required_providers {
    azurerm = {
      source  = "hashicorp/azurerm"
      version = "=2.53.0"
    }
  }

  required_version = "~> 0.14"
}

provider "azurerm" {
  features {}
}

variable resource_group_name { type=list(string) }

output stringdsingleline {
    value = "%{ for val in var.resource_group_name } ${ val } %{ endfor }"
}
```

The configuration accepts a single parameter resource_group_name of type list(string). The output from the configuration is derived from a string directive. The whole expression is within double quotes just like string interpolation. The first part of the string directive defined using %{...} declares a "for" loop, iterating through the values in list collection(var.resource_group_name). The next part of the expression is simply accesses and returns the current value in the collection, and the part %{ endfor } terminates the loop once all the items in the collection are iterated. The values within the collection can be accessing using the syntax and the whole {} is repeated for the number of elements available within the collection.

If this configuration is executed with the command line, as shown next,

```
terraform apply -var='resource_group_name=["rgfirst", "rgsecond", "rgthird"]'
```

it will result in the output shown in Figure 4-12.

Apply complete! Resources: 0 added, 0 changed, 0 destroyed.

Outputs:

```
stringdsingleline = " rgfirst  rgsecond  rgthird "
```

Figure 4-12. *Terraform string directive usage*

Notice the whitespaces in output from execution. Anything defined within the opening %{..} and %{endfor} is evaluated as is, preserving the whitespaces and line feeds.

The next shown output element has a string directive that does not have whitespace between the start and end statements of for loop. Notice that there is no whitespace before and after ${} syntax.

```
output stringdsingleline {
    value = "%{ for val in var.resource_group_name }${ val }%{ endfor }"
}
```

The output from previous configuration will have no whitespaces between the values, as shown in Figure 4-13.

Apply complete! Resources: 0 added, 0 changed, 0 destroyed.

Outputs:

```
stringdsingleline = "rgfirstrgsecondrgthird"
```

Figure 4-13. *Terraform string directive usage with no whitespace*

String directives can also be specified within string values spanning multiple lines known as *here-docs*. The rules for string directives in here-docs are the same as for general strings defined in a single line. The following code is an example of a string directive with a here-doc:

```
terraform {
  required_providers {
    azurerm = {
      source  = "hashicorp/azurerm"
      version = "=2.53.0"
    }
  }

  required_version = "~> 0.14"
}

provider "azurerm" {
  features {}
}

variable resource_group_name { type=list(string) }

output stringd {
    value = <<EOT
    %{ for val in var.resource_group_name }
    ${ val }
    %{ endfor }
    EOT
}
```

The output from the previous configuration execution is also a here-doc. Here-docs in Terraform are defined using "<<EOT" and "EOT" tags. Both the beginning <<EOT and ending EOT should be on separate lines. The code in a here-doc is the same as that in the previous example, and the output is also the same. It is just another way of authoring more readable configuration along with usage of string directives.

String directives also support conditional statements and executions. "If-else-endif" statements are provided in Terraform as part of string directives to support conditional statements. Each of these should be within the %{..} operators. Anything defined within them will be evaluated and returned as a string. Depending on the evaluation value return for conditional statement either the "if" or the "else" section of the code is executed. Here's an example:

```
terraform {
  required_providers {
    azurerm = {
      source  = "hashicorp/azurerm"
      version = "=2.53.0"
    }
  }

  required_version = "~> 0.14"
}

provider "azurerm" {
  features {}
}

variable resource_group_name { type=list(string) }

output ifstringdirective {
    value = "%{ if var.resource_group_name == "simpletfexample" } name
    of resource group is ${ var.resource_group_name } %{else} improper
    resource group name %{ endif }"

}
```

Terraform Functions

Terraform provides a rich set of built-in functions. Each function performs a specific task and they can be used anywhere within a Terraform expression. There are more than 100 functions in Terraform and you can learn more about them at https://www.terraform.io/docs/language/functions/index.html.

Functions are invoked using their names along with appropriate expected parameters. A function invocation syntax involves the function name along with its parameters in brackets.

```
functionname(parameter1, parameter2, ... )
```

The following is an example of invoking a function from an expression:

```
Split(',',  "rgname1, rgname2, rgname3" )
```

The `split` function accepts a delimiter as its first parameter and string value as second parameter that should be split based on the delimiter.

It is not possible to cover all the functions within this book, but some of the major ones will be covered along with their usage through examples in other sections. The functions fall into these categories:

- *Numeric functions*: These functions help perform numeric calculations such as finding maximum or minimum values from a set collection.

- *String functions*: These functions help perform string manipulation such as splitting and replacing string values.

- *Collection functions*: These functions are applied on collection types such as sets, lists, and maps to join, concatenate, slice, and others.

- *Encoding functions*: These functions help in encoding strings into JSON, YAML, base64, and vice versa.

- *Filesystem functions*: These functions help in file handling capabilities from within Terraform expressions.

- *Date and time functions*: These functions help in data and time manipulation such as adding time, getting current timestamps, and more.

- *Hash and crypto functions*: These functions help in generating hashes using a different algorithm from the provided inputs.

- *IP network functions*: These functions help work with IP addresses and subnet ranges.

- *Type conversion function*: These functions help in converting from one datatype to another.

In next section, we will understand the concept of provisioners in Terraform and how they help in extending any resource capability.

Provisioners

Terraform is based on an extensible architecture and can be extended with additional plugins and providers. However, not all requirements demand writing new plugins and providers. There are requirements where we might need to execute additional logic apart from the logic already provided by an existing resource. To execute this additional logic, Terraform provides the concept of *provisioners* to help automate and execute scripts as part of an existing resource. There is no need to modify the existing providers; instead, provisioner blocks can be injected into any resource and executed as part of the resource configuration.

A provisioner block has its own set of attributes. A provisioner block consists of the keyword `"provisioner"` along with the type of provisioner. Terraform provides three types of built-in provisioners, and it is possible to create custom provisioners as well.

The built-in provisioners are as follows:

- **file**: This provisioner helps in copying files from the machine running Terraform to the target resource. For example, a file provisioner could be associated with an `azurerm_virtual_machine` resource, and based on the provisioner configuration, it would copy files and folders to a remote virtual machine from a local machine executing the Terraform configuration. The resource should be capable of accepting the file from the local machine.

- **local-exec**: This provisioner helps in executing scripts based on multiple scripting languages on the local machine executing the Terraform configuration. It supports Bash, PowerShell, Perl, or any other scripting language available on the machine.

- **remote-exec**: This provisioner helps in executing scripts on the resources it is associated with. They are generally associated with virtual machine and virtual machine scale set resources. The remote resource should be capable of executing the scripts and commands provided by the `remote-exec` provisioner.

local-exec

The declaration of the local-exec block consists of four attributes, out of which only "command" is a mandatory attribute and the rest are optional. The optional attributes are "working_dir", "interpreter", and "environment".

The value assigned to command attribute is either a path to a script file or a CLI command itself.

The working_dir attribute is the reference to the local current working directory path that acts as context for command execution. It generally contains files and folders on which the script is dependent on.

The interpreter attribute helps in determining the scripting tool and language that will be used for execution of the command and scripts. It is an optional attribute and if not used, the operating system's preferred scripting tool is used for execution. For example, the interpreter will default to PowerShell on Windows and similarly to bash on Linux operating system.

The environment attribute helps add the environmental variables that the executing script might require.

An example of local-exec is shown next. In this example, a provisioner is associated with resource group resource. It executes the "deploy.sh" script file located at the ./path/to/scripts directory with Bash and also declares a couple of environment variables.

```
resource "azurerm_resource_group" "resource_group" {
  name     = var.resource_group_name
  location = var.resource_group_location

  provisioner "local-exec" {
    command = "deploy.sh"
    working_dir = "./path/to/scripts"
    interpreter = ["bash", "-c"]
    environment = {
      ENVVAR1 = "envvar1 value"
      ENVVAR2 = "envvar2 value"
    }
  }
}
```

Using local-exec in Terraform Configuration

In this section, a new resource group will be defined within the Terraform configuration to understand the usage of provisioners within resources. The resource group configuration will also have a local-exec provisioner associated with it. It will simply execute a Bash "echo" command that accesses properties of the resource group.

There could be a need to execute a script as part of the overall configuration, and the script might not be associated with any particular resource. In such cases, Terraform provides "null_resource", available from the "null" provider. It does not provision any resource but provides a placeholder and helps in executing scripts using provisioners. Note that terraform init should be executed every time there is a change in configuration with resources from new provider. The command for the provisioner in null_resource just executes the bash date command. The interpreter invokes the bash interpreter and passes the commands to command attribute.

```
terraform {
  required_providers {
    azurerm = {
      source  = "hashicorp/azurerm"
      version = "=2.53.0"
    }
  }

  required_version = "~> 0.14"
}

provider "azurerm" {
  features {}
}

variable resource_group_name { type= string }
variable resource_group_location { type= string }

resource "azurerm_resource_group" "resource_group" {
  name     = var.resource_group_name
  location = var.resource_group_location

  provisioner "local-exec" {
```

```
   command = "echo ${azurerm_resource_group.resource_group.id}"
  }
}

resource "null_resource" mynullresource {
    provisioner "local-exec" {
      command  = "date"
      interpreter = ["bash", "-c"]
    }
  }
```

The configuration can be executed using the following command:

```
terraform apply -var='resource_group_name=provisionerexec' -var='resource_
group_location=westus'
```

The result displays both the date-time from the date command and the resource group identifier from the echo command, as shown in Figure 4-14.

```
null_resource.mynullresource: Creating...
null_resource.mynullresource: Provisioning with 'local-exec'...
null_resource.mynullresource (local-exec): Executing: ["bash" "-c" "date"]
null_resource.mynullresource (local-exec): Tue 15 Jun 2021 23:07:07 IST
null_resource.mynullresource: Creation complete after 0s [id=2773231966771128036]
azurerm_resource_group.resource_group: Creating...
azurerm_resource_group.resource_group: Provisioning with 'local-exec'...
azurerm_resource_group.resource_group (local-exec): Executing: ["/bin/sh" "-c" "echo /subscriptions/9755ffce-e94b-4332-9be8-1ade15e78909/resourceGroups/provisionerexec"]
azurerm_resource_group.resource_group (local-exec): /subscriptions/9755ffce-e94b-4332-9be8-1ade15e78909/resourceGroups/provisionerexec
azurerm_resource_group.resource_group: Creation complete after 2s [id=/subscriptions/9755ffce-e94b-4332-9be8-1ade15e78909/resourceGroups/provisionerexec]

Apply complete! Resources: 2 added, 0 changed, 0 destroyed.
```

Figure 4-14. *Terraform output displaying usage of local-exec*

As mentioned before, scripts can also be executed as part of the command attribute and is shown next. The deploy.sh script is executed as part of the execution of provisioner.

```
provisioner "local-exec" { command = "/bin/bash deploy.sh" }
```

It is possible to define multiple local-exec provisioners within a single resource, and they get executed in the order of their appearance.

By default, the provisioners are executed at the creation time of the resource, i.e., when the parent resource gets provisioned. It is also possible to execute a provisioner to execute during the destroy time of the parent resource. This is shown in the next code listing.

The only difference in the code listing shown next from the previous listing is the addition of the "when" attribute. It accepts "destroy" as a value, and that ensures the provisioner will execute as part of the destroy operation on the resource.

```terraform
terraform {
  required_providers {
    azurerm = {
      source  = "hashicorp/azurerm"
      version = "=2.53.0"
    }
  }

  required_version = "~> 0.14"
}

provider "azurerm" {
  features {}
}

variable resource_group_name { type= string }
variable resource_group_location { type= string }

resource "azurerm_resource_group" "resource_group" {
  name     = var.resource_group_name
  location = var.resource_group_location

  provisioner "local-exec" {
    command = "echo ${azurerm_resource_group.resource_group.id}"
  }
}

resource "null_resource" mynullresource {
    provisioner "local-exec" {
      when = "destroy"
      command  = "date"
      interpreter = ["bash", "-c"]
    }
}
```

The command used to destroy the previously created resource group and configuration is shown next. Notice the addition of the `destroy` options toward the end of the command.

```
terraform apply -var='resource_group_name=provisionerexec' -var='resource_group_location=westus' -destroy
```

This time the result consists of the date output; however, it does not do an echo of the resource group identifier. This is because the resource group identifier is echoed during the provisioning of the resource, while `date` is part of the output during the `destroy` operation, as shown in Figure 4-15.

```
null_resource.mynullresource: Destroying... [id=4764139794129882380]
null_resource.mynullresource: Provisioning with 'local-exec'...
null_resource.mynullresource (local-exec): Executing: ["bash" "-c" "date"]
null_resource.mynullresource (local-exec): Tue 15 Jun 2021 22:55:06 IST
null_resource.mynullresource: Destruction complete after 0s
azurerm_resource_group.resource_group: Destroying... [id=/subscriptions/9755ffce-e94b-4332-9be8-1ade15e78909/resourceGroups/provisionerexec]
azurerm_resource_group.resource_group: Still destroying... [id=/subscriptions/9755ffce-e94b-4332-9be8-...5e78909/resourceGroups/provisionerexec, 10s elapsed]
azurerm_resource_group.resource_group: Still destroying... [id=/subscriptions/9755ffce-e94b-4332-9be8-...5e78909/resourceGroups/provisionerexec, 20s elapsed]
azurerm_resource_group.resource_group: Still destroying... [id=/subscriptions/9755ffce-e94b-4332-9be8-...5e78909/resourceGroups/provisionerexec, 30s elapsed]
azurerm_resource_group.resource_group: Still destroying... [id=/subscriptions/9755ffce-e94b-4332-9be8-...5e78909/resourceGroups/provisionerexec, 40s elapsed]
azurerm_resource_group.resource_group: Still destroying... [id=/subscriptions/9755ffce-e94b-4332-9be8-...5e78909/resourceGroups/provisionerexec, 50s elapsed]
azurerm_resource_group.resource_group: Destruction complete after 51s

Apply complete! Resources: 0 added, 0 changed, 2 destroyed.
```

Figure 4-15. *Terraform output displaying usage of null-resource*

The `terraform apply` command fails when the command or script from provisioning encounters an error. This default execution can be modified such that the application of the configuration does not fail in case an error arises from the provisioners. There is an additional meta-attribute called `"on_failure"` that can be added to the provisioner configuration. It can take `"fail"` or `"continue"` as its value. `fail` is the default value, and assigning `continue` to this attribute will ensure that the configuration does not fail even if the provisioner encounters an error.

File Provisioner

As mentioned, the file provisioner helps in copying folders and files to the target resource, and the resource should have the capability to accept the incoming file. Not all resources have this capability, and only resources such as virtual machines and virtual machine scale sets are capable of accepting and storing the files.

The file provisioner declaration is shown next. It copies the `deploywebserver.conf` file from the machine running Terraform to the `/etc` directory on the resource.

```
provisioner "file" {
  source      = "conf/deploywebserver.conf"
  destination = "/etc"
}
```

remote-exec

`remote-exec` provisioners execute scripts and commands on remote resources. The resource should be capable of executing the commands and scripts. Typically, virtual machines and virtual machine scale sets have this capability.

A `remote-exec` block is similar to a `local-exec` block and is shown here:

```
provisioner "remote-exec" {
  inline = [
    "Terraform init",
    "Terraform apply",
  ]
}
```

`remote-exec` accepts three mutually exclusive attributes. The inline attribute accepts a list of commands to execute on the remote resource in order of declaration.

`remote-exec` also accepts a `script` attribute that will copy the file from machine running Terraform to remote resource and execute it. It accepts a path to a single file.

`remote-exec` also has a `scripts` attribute and is similar to a `script` attribute with the only difference that it accepts multiple script files, and they are executed one after another in order of declaration.

Summary

Terraform is a versatile tool for provisioning and managing infrastructure. For authoring rich configurations, Terraform provides capabilities that can help in iterating over collections and generating resources dynamically, all within a single block using the count attribute. The same capability with a difference nuance is provided by the for_each attribute. for_each works not only at the resource level but also at the resource property levels. This makes authoring Terraform configuration more manageable and readable. Terraform provides rich string manipulation capabilities including string directives and string interpolation. It also provides multiple built-in functions to help in authoring generic and feature-rich configurations. Terraform programmability is based on expressions, and expressions are evaluated at runtime. They provide runtime behavior and generate output that can then become part of the configuration. Terraform provides provisioners that can help execute scripts both locally as well as remotely and can help execute any logic possible through these scripts. It opens up a world of different implementation opportunities with Terraform. In the next chapter, we will delve into the world of Terraform modules, implementing them and creating reusable and generic Terraform scripts.

CHAPTER 5

Terraform Modules

Terraform helps to automate infrastructure management using HCL scripts. HCL, as you know by now, is a declarative-based language comprising resource declaration and configuration. The scripts consist of root configuration and is the starting point of script execution. The root configuration can declare provider specific resources directly or instead they can use modules. Terraform provides modules that are essential building blocks for resources and the overall solution. Modules are Terraform scripts that are sourced from an external location and combined with the root configuration. Modules do not have the root configuration and are meant to be used within the root configuration. Modules solve some of the important infrastructure as code (IaC) issues such as reusability, standardization, uniformity, and consistency in deployments across environments, solutions, and teams.

This chapter will cover the following:

- Module overview

- Authoring modules

- Testing modules

- Publishing and consuming modules

Overview

Terraform CLI commands generally uses a folder as scope consisting of Terraform files for deployment. The Terraform configuration within a folder can comprise a single file consisting or can be broken down into multiple files—each file consisting of a subset of Terraform script that conceptually belongs together.

© Ritesh Modi 2021
R. Modi, *Deep-Dive Terraform on Azure*, https://doi.org/10.1007/978-1-4842-7328-9_5

We have seen the breaking down of monolith Terraform files into:

- The Terraform, provider, and versioning configurations.

- The `locals` configuration can be put in another file.

- The `variables`, `locals`, and `output` blocks are each in their own file.

- Resources and data are also in different files.

Terraform CLI commands like `apply` and `plan` combine these files before executing them. From the Terraform execution perspective, there is no difference whether the configuration blocks are in a single file or in multiple files. They are eventually combined before execution by the Terraform commands. The main advantage of authoring Terraform scripts into multiple files is easy authoring, extensibility, and maintenance of scripts as they keep increasing in size and complexity over a period of time.

Breaking a large Terraform file into smaller logical files is one step toward better maintainability and extensibility; however, it does not solve all the challenges. There are other challenges in terms of reusability, sharing, and duplication of code. We'll cover these aspects in a bit more detail in the next section.

Modules are no different in terms of authoring and execution perspective. A module is a folder consisting of Terraform files with the definition and configuration of resources. It accepts values for variables and generates output. Almost every element available in Terraform can be used within a module. So, what is the difference between a module and a Terraform script?

Terraform modules cannot be executed on their own. They need a main Terraform script or root configuration to be executed. They do not have their own configuration related to the backend state.

Why Do We Need Modules?

Terraform scripts are used to provision multiple types of environments like development, staging, and production environment and deploying them using module provides benefits in terms of uniformity, reusability and governance.

Uniformity

Terraform state files are core to how Terraform deployments work. The state file is generated for each root configuration. The root configurations are defined at the folder level, and any script within a folder becomes part of the root configuration. Modules help in standardizing the resources and developers can use module to declare resources in uniformity. With multiple environments for each solution, Terraform developers have to author resources for each environment. Even multiple resources of the same type are sometimes needed for an environment. Terraform developers in a team will often configure resources of the same type in different ways. This could lead to nonuniformity within the code. With modules in place, instead of authoring resources directly, the developers refer to modules for the creation of resources. The modules remain the same for all the developers and solutions. This ensures that each resource is defined uniformly across teams.

Reusability

A module contains resources that can be applied across projects, solutions, and teams. This ensures that developers need not spend time on configuring resources directly for Terraform configurations; rather, they can reuse modules and configure them as part of the solution. This also ensures that resources can be standardized at the module level, and all resources that are part of modules are configured equivalently.

Applying Policies

Terraform resources can be directly authored within the root configuration. Doing so allows developers to configure the resource as they deem necessary. It does not enforce any policy or governance on the resources. Modules can be authored with constraints and rules that best suit the organization and solution. For example, adding organization-level tags to resources, constraining the resource deployment region, etc., can be implemented as part of the module. Using the module will ensure that those tags are automatically added to the resource in case the developer misses using them. Similarly, other custom policies can be developed within the module, and all resources will adhere to them during deployment.

Structure of a Module

A module essentially is a folder or directory comprised of Terraform scripts. The main difference between a general script and a module is that a general script can be executed using Terraform CLI commands, and the modules cannot be executed directly using the Terraform commands. The modules are like a library that needs a main script that can be executed using a Terraform command and uses modules as part of its script.

Modules typically comprise one or more resources logically grouped together and these resources are represented as a single unit. Provisioning a module would mean provisioning all its resources.

A module cannot be executed on its own and should be used by the main Terraform script to provision its resources.

Figure 5-1 shows a project that encompasses the use of modules.

Figure 5-1. *Terraform folder structure with modules*

This is just a suggestive folder structure based on best practices and easier authoring and maintenance of Terraform scripts. It can be extended with additional folders and files depending on the scale, size, and complexity of the solution and can include a `services` folder under the `modules` folder. The `services` folder would group multiple modules together to form a *service*. Eventually all services could roll up to form a *solution*. Services have not been included in this book in the interest of brevity. See Figure 5-2 for understanding a possible module hierarchy.

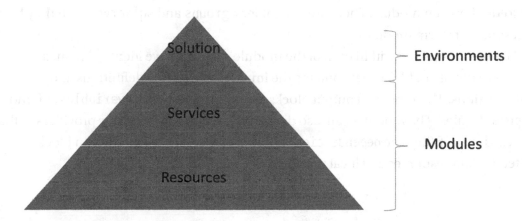

Figure 5-2. *Module hierarchy*

Resources are base-level modules. Resource modules comprise resources at the lowest level. They contain resources made available by the Terraform providers. Modules can contain a single resource or a group of resources that have same lifecycle, are closely associated, and are provisioned/deprovisioned together. Examples of a module consisting of multiple resources would be Cosmos DB database and collection or a Blob storage account along with a container. Resources at this level are represented as technical building blocks that have no notion how they would be consumed within an overall solution or service.

The resource modules roll up to create service modules. Services are higher-level building blocks compared to resource modules. A service module brings together multiple resource modules, composed in a meaningful manner to provision infrastructure for services. These services are the main components within the overall solution. An example of services for a web application would be front-end and back-end services. The front-end service would be comprised of multiple modules such as the app service plan, web app, application insights, and web app configuration, while the backend service would comprise the SQL Server module.

A solution will bring together multiple services to provision the infrastructure required for the solution.

Developing a Module

The previous section showed the overall folder structure for a Terraform solution using modules. The `modules` folder has `resources` subfolder. The `resources` folder contains one folder for each module. There are two folders, `groups` and `sqlserver`, and they both represent Terraform modules.

The files contained within each of the module's folders have identical names. They have the `main.tf` file that contains the important resource definitions and configurations. The input and output blocks are defined within the `variables.tf` and `outputs.tf` files. The modules can also declare the required version for providers within the `versions.tf` file. The `dependencies.tf` file is empty, and it can contain blocks related to data resources and local variables. See Figure 5-3.

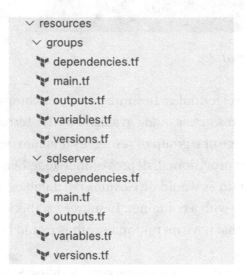

Figure 5-3. *Folder structure for modules*

Each module can also declare its dependency on the provider version number. This informs the user of the module to use a compatible version in root configuration.

The code files associated with this chapter consist of two modules: the resource group and SQL Server. The resource group module provisions a single resource group. This is an example of a module with a single resource. The SQL Server module comprises of three resources: SQL Server, SQL database, and Azure SQL firewall rules.

The versions file of each module has a Terraform block, and it defines the required version for the providers it is dependent on. The current modules are dependent on the version 2.51.0 of the azurerm provider. This is shown here:

```
terraform {
  required_providers {
    azurerm = {
      source  = "hashicorp/azurerm"
      version = "=2.51.0"
    }
  }
}
```

The main.tf file contains the resource definitions of the module. It consists of resources that are composed together along with their configurations. The configuration values can utilize local and input variables. They can also be dependent on configuration values from other resources.

Resource Group Module

The code listing shown next defines a resource group configuration using the azurerm_resource_group resource. The configuration gets values for its name, location, and tags attributes from the input variables.

```
resource azurerm_resource_group resourceGroup {
    name = var.resourceGroupName
    location = var.resourceGroupLocation

    tags = var.resourceGroupTags
}
```

The input variables are defined within the `variables.tf` file, which consists of the same three variables needed by resources defined in the `main.tf` file.

```
variable resourceGroupName { type= string}
variable resourceGroupLocation { type= string}
variable resourceGroupTags { type =  map(string)}
```

The output variable consists of values generated as output from Terraform execution. The output can consist of single values as represented by resource group identifier, resource group location, resource group name, and resource group tags, or it might consist of complete runtime resource configuration information as in the case of the complete resource group output variable. The complete output variables are especially helpful in unit testing since it provides complete configuration values for a resource to test with the expected values.

```
output "completeResourceGroup" {
    value = azurerm_resource_group.resourceGroup
}

output "resourceGroupIdentifier" {
    value = azurerm_resource_group.resourceGroup.id
}

output "resourceGroupName" {
    value = azurerm_resource_group.resourceGroup.name
}

output "resourceGroupTags" {
    value = azurerm_resource_group.resourceGroup.tags
}

output "resourceGroupLocation" {
    value = azurerm_resource_group.resourceGroup.location
}
```

SQL Server Module

The SQL Server module is comparatively a bigger module than the resource group module. It contains three resources that are created and maintained together and share the same lifecycle. It also has a declared dependence on a specific version of the `azurerm` provider and utilizes of input and output variables. It first creates an Azure SQL Server resource followed by SQL firewall rules and SQL database. Both the SQL firewall and SQL database have dependence on Azure SQL Server, and this implicit dependence is set by ensuring that these resources use the runtime resource property values to assign to their `server_name` attribute. The next code listing shows the code for the `main.tf` file consisting of all three resources. These resources are supported by input variables.

```
resource "azurerm_sql_server" "sql_server" {
  name = var.sql_server_name

  location            = var.location
  resource_group_name = var.resource_group_name

  version                      = "12.0"
  administrator_login          = var.admin_username
  administrator_login_password = var.admin_password

  tags = var.sql_tags
}

resource "azurerm_sql_firewall_rule" "sql_firewall_rule" {
  count = length(var.whitelist_ip_addresses)

  name                = "iprule-${count.index}"
  resource_group_name = var.resource_group_name
  server_name         = azurerm_sql_server.sql_server.name

  start_ip_address = cidrhost(var.whitelist_ip_addresses[count.index], 0)
  end_ip_address   = cidrhost(var.whitelist_ip_addresses[count.index], -1)
}
```

```
resource "azurerm_sql_database" "sql_database" {

  name                 = var.database_name
  location             = var.location
  resource_group_name  = var.resource_group_name

  server_name = azurerm_sql_server.sql_server.name
  collation   = "SQL_LATIN1_GENERAL_CP1_CI_AS"

  requested_service_objective_name = "S2"

  tags = var.sql_tags
}
```

The variables for the SQL Server module are shown here:

```
variable "resource_group_name" {
  description = "name of resource group for hosting sql server and
database"
  type = string
}

variable "location" {
  description = "Azure region for resource group and sql resources"
  type        = string
}

variable "whitelist_ip_addresses" {
  description = "whitelist ip address for sql server"
  type        = list(string)
  default     = ["0.0.0.0/32"]
}

variable "sql_server_name" {
  description = "sql server display and internal name"
  type        = string
}
```

```
variable "admin_username" {
  description = "admin username associated with sql server"
  type        = string
}

variable "admin_password" {
  description = "admin password associated with sql server"
  type        = string
}

variable "database_name" {
  description = "sql database display and internal name"
  type        = string
}

variable "sql_tags" {
  type = map(string)
}
```

The output variables from the SQL Server module are listed next:

```
output "sql_server_id" {
  description = "Id of the SQL Server"
  value       = azurerm_sql_server.sql_server.id
}

output "sql_server_fqdn" {
  description = "Fully qualified domain name of the SQL Server"
  value       = azurerm_sql_server.sql_server.fully_qualified_domain_name
}

output "sql_databases_id" {
  description = "Id of the SQL Databases"
  value       = azurerm_sql_database.sql_database.id
}
```

Now with a couple of modules already developed, it is a good practice to test them before consuming them in other Terraform configurations. The next sections provide a simple way to test Terraform modules. We'll look at unit testing Terraform scripts using the TerraTest framework written in Golang.

Testing a Module

You know by now that a standalone module cannot be executed on its own. It needs a root configuration to execute it. So far, we have been able to create a couple of modules, and the next logical step is to enable testing of these modules. We'll also see examples of how to use modules from the root configuration.

A subdirectory named `fixtures` is part of the `modules` folder. It has two folders, one for each module. They are even named with the same names as the `modules` folder name. These folders contain a root configuration for each module. Executing these fixtures will result in consuming modules and thereby help to test modules. These fixtures for each module can also act as usage examples for the module. See Figure 5-4.

Figure 5-4. *Folder structure for fixtures related to modules*

The fixtures declare the `terraform` and `required_provider` configurations along with the module declaration and its input and output variables.

The `main.tf` file contains a module block responsible for consuming the resource group module, as shown next:

```
terraform {
  required_providers {
    azurerm = {
      source  = "hashicorp/azurerm"
      version = "=2.51.0"
    }
  }
}

provider "azurerm" {
    features {}
}
```

```
module "resource_group" {
    source = "../../resources/groups"
    resourceGroupName = var.resourceGroupName
    resourceGroupLocation = var.resourceGroupLocation
    resourceGroupTags = var.resourceGroupTags
}
```

The resource group module expects three variables: resource group name, resource group location, and resource group tags. These variables are declared within the variables.tf file along with their data types.

```
variable resourceGroupName { type= string}
variable resourceGroupLocation { type= string}
variable resourceGroupTags { type =  map(string)}
```

The resource group module outputs five output variables. These are captured in fixtures to output all the outputs from the module.

```
output "completeResourceGroup" {
    value = module.resource_group.completeResourceGroup
}

output "resourceGroupIdentifier" {
    value = module.resource_group.resourceGroupIdentifier
}

output "resourceGroupName" {
    value = module.resource_group.resourceGroupName
}

output "resourceGroupTags" {
    value = module.resource_group.resourceGroupTags
}

output "resourceGroupLocation" {
    value = module.resource_group.resourceGroupLocation
}
```

Now that we know the process of creating modules and testing them, it's time to use them in another Terraform configuration. The process and details are explained in the next section.

Using a Module

Modules can be consumed in Terraform scripts by making them part of the configuration. Just as resources are declared and used within Terraform, Terraform provides the module block along with its identifier. The only mandatory attribute for a module block is the source attribute. The source attribute defines the location of the module from which it should download its definition and provision resources. Additionally, and optionally, the module block accepts the values for the variables needed for the working of the module.

An example of a module that provisions a resource group and accepts three variables (resource group name, resource group location, and resource group tags) is shown here:

```
module "resourceGroup" {
    source  = "../../modules/resources/groups"
    resourceGroupName = var.resourceGroupName
    resourceGroupLocation = var.resourceGroupLocation
    resourceGroupTags = var.resourceGroupTags

}
```

Notice the way the source attribute is provided with a local relative path value to the module. The module keyword is followed by an identifier through which this module can be referenced in the local code. The block has a source and variables accepted by the module as attributes.

Modules are plugins that are downloaded and installed in the local .terraform folder managed by Terraform at the time of executing the terraform init command. The terraform init command initializes the modules after downloading it, and then it configures the local or remote backend alongside the plugins (providers) used within the configuration.

```
MININT-AUQ808G:environments riteshmodi$ terraform init
Initializing modules...

Initializing the backend...

Initializing provider plugins...
- Reusing previous version of hashicorp/azurerm from the dependency lock file
- Using previously-installed hashicorp/azurerm v2.51.0

Terraform has been successfully initialized!

You may now begin working with Terraform. Try running "terraform plan" to see
any changes that are required for your infrastructure. All Terraform commands
should now work.

If you ever set or change modules or backend configuration for Terraform,
rerun this command to reinitialize your working directory. If you forget, other
commands will detect it and remind you to do so if necessary.
```

The references to the module for a Terraform deployment are stored within the modules folder of the .terraform directory. The is Terraform's internal directory and should not be edited. Terraform uses the modules.json file to store the references and uses it to identify the modules, their sources, and the name of the module. See Figure 5-5.

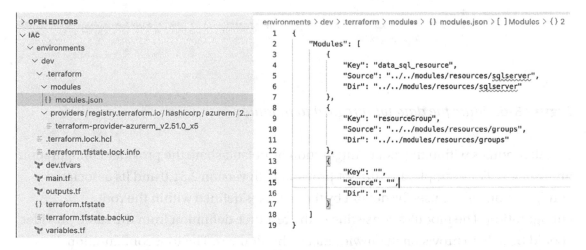

Figure 5-5. *Terraform modules.json file with module declarations*

It is important to note that the module configuration is not stored within the .terraform directory. Instead, just like resources, input variables, and output variables, Terraform stored the module configuration within the state file. The state file has one section per resource whether the resource is provisioned directly or through a module. For each resource in a module, the module name (both in the source module and the name provided in the local script), the type of resource, the provider, and the resource configuration are stored within the state file. Figure 5-6 shows the snippet related to the resource group module.

```
{
    "module": "module.resourceGroup",
    "mode": "managed",
    "type": "azurerm_resource_group",
    "name": "resourceGroup",
    "provider": "provider[\"registry.terraform.io/hashicorp/azurerm\"]",
    "instances": [
        {
            "schema_version": 0,
            "attributes": {
                "id": "/subscriptions/8e0502bf-56ff-4d96-81e7-11725e8065dd/resourceGroups/dev-rgFinance",
                "location": "westeurope",
                "name": "dev-rgFinance",
                "tags": {
                    "department": "finance",
                    "environment": "development",
                    "owner": "ritesh modi"
                },
                "timeouts": null
            },
            "sensitive_attributes": [],
            "private":
            "eyJlMmJmYjczMC1lY2FhLTExZTYtOGY4OC0zNDM2M2JjN2M0YzAiOnsiY3JlYXRlIjo1NDAwMDAwMDAwMDAwLCJkZW
            kYXRlIjo1NDAwMDAwMDAwMDAwfX0="
        }
    ]
}
```

Figure 5-6. *State file data with regard to modules*

All modules within the root configuration by default share the provider configuration and version. For example, an azurerm provider with version 2.51.0 and its associated configuration will be used by default by the modules defined within the root configuration. The modules consisting of the resource definition from the same provider should be able to provision them without any hindrances. The root configuration can have multiple declared providers of the same type, and the modules can then be associated with any one of the providers by adding the providers block within the module.

The code for the dev environment using modules as an example is shown next. The script for dev environment is similar to code we saw earlier for writing fixtures, with the difference that both the resource group and SQL Server modules are consumed together from within the root configuration. Azure CLI login command is used to for authentication, and `azurerm_client_config` data source ensures that the same credentials are used by Terraform to authenticate with Azure. Both the resource group and SQL Server module are referenced using the `source` attribute with the local path as its value.

```
terraform {
  required_providers {
    azurerm = {
      source  = "hashicorp/azurerm"
      version = "=2.51.0"
    }
  }
}

provider "azurerm" {
    features {}
}

data "azurerm_client_config" "current" {}
module "resourceGroup" {
    source  = "../../modules/resources/groups"
    resourceGroupName = var.resourceGroupName
    resourceGroupLocation = var.resourceGroupLocation
    resourceGroupTags = var.resourceGroupTags

}

module "data_sql_resource" {
    source  = "../../modules/resources/sqlserver"
    resource_group_name = module.resourceGroup.resourceGroupName
    location = var.resourceGroupLocation
    whitelist_ip_addresses = var.whitelist_ip_addresses
    sql_server_name = var.sql_server_name
    admin_username = var.admin_username
    admin_password = var.admin_password
    database_name = var.database_name
    sql_tags = var.sql_tags
}
```

Each environment declares the input variables required by the root configuration, some of which are eventually supplied to the modules. This is shown in the next code listing:

```
variable resourceGroupName { type= string}
variable resourceGroupLocation { type= string}

variable resourceGroupTags { type =  map(string)}

variable "sql_tags" {
    type = map(string)
}

variable "whitelist_ip_addresses" {
  description = "whitelist ip address for sql server"
  type        = list(string)
  default     = ["0.0.0.0/32"]
}

variable "sql_server_name" {
  description = "sql server display and internal name"
  type        = string
}

variable "admin_username" {
  description = "admin username associated with sql server"
  type        = string
}

variable "admin_password" {
  description = "admin password associated with sql server"
  type        = string
}

variable "database_name" {
  description = "sql database display and internal name"
  type        = string
}
```

The outputs.tf file contains the outputs from the root configuration, and it refers to the outputs from modules within the configuration as well. This is shown in the next code listing:

```
output "completeResourceGroup" {
    value = module.resourceGroup.completeResourceGroup
}

output "resourceGroupIdentifier" {
    value = module.resourceGroup.resourceGroupIdentifier
}

output "resourceGroupName" {
    value = module.resourceGroup.resourceGroupName
}

output "resourceGroupLocation" {
    value = module.resourceGroup.resourceGroupLocation
}

output "sql_server_id" {
  description = "Id of the SQL Server"
  value       = module.data_sql_resource.sql_server_id
}

output "sql_server_fqdn" {
  description = "Fully qualified domain name of the SQL Server"
  value       = module.data_sql_resource.sql_server_fqdn
}

output "sql_databases_id" {
  description = "Id of the SQL Databases"
  value       = module.data_sql_resource.sql_databases_id
}
```

Each environment declares input variables, and they must be supplied during deployment time. Terraform provides multiple ways to supply values to input variables. Nonsensitive and general input values can be supplied using a dedicated variables file containing these values. This file has .tfvars as its extension. The input variables gets mapped to variable values defined in the .tfvars file during execution. The values for variables defined in the dev.tfvars file (for development environment) is shown in the next code listing. Each environment should have its own .tfvars file containing values specific to that environment.

```
resourceGroupName = "dev-rgFinance"
resourceGroupLocation = "west europe"
resourceGroupTags = {
    "department" = "finance",
    "environment" = "development",
    "owner" = "ritesh modi"
}

whitelist_ip_addresses = ["0.0.0.0/32"]
sql_server_name = "uniquesqlname"
admin_username = "sqlusername"
admin_password = "asdseqsdfa123.."
database_name = "employees"
sql_tags = {
    "department" = "finance",
    "environment" = "development",
    "owner" = "ritesh modi"
}
```

Although publishing the module is optional (a module can be consumed using its local path), it is a good practice to publish the modules to either public or private repositories for further consumption in other solutions and projects.

Publishing Module

Modules can be consumed from a variety of sources. The modules created so far were part of the same solution and so the modules could be referenced using a relative path to the module. Just to reiterate, the source attribute to the resource group module has a path value relative to the current folder.

```
source  = "../../modules/resources/groups"
```

This is just one of the ways to refer to a module out of the myriad ways provided by Terraform.

Terraform modules can be published to the Terraform registry. The Terraform registry is a public centralized location of modules and providers managed and maintained by creators of Terraform. It provides full support for versioning and a native way of publishing modules. The form to uniquely identify a module in the Terraform registry is as follows:

```
<Namespace>/<Name>/<Provider>
```

An example of consuming a module from the Terraform registry is shown next. This module is responsible for managing Azure networks.

Source = "Azure/network/azurerm"

The namespace is Azure, `azurerm` is the provider, and `network` is the name of the module. Similarly, the module published at "`Azure/compute/azurerm`" helps in managing virtual machines:

Source = "Azure/compute/azurerm"

The provider and namespace name remains `azurerm` and `Azure`, respectively, and the name of module is `compute` in this case.

All modules related to Azure in the Terraform registry are available at `https://registry.terraform.io/namespaces/Azure`.

Terraform modules can be published in versioning controlled repositories like GitHub, Bitbucket and even Azure storage accounts.

The GitHub source should contain the path to the module without the protocol information. The following is an example of a GitHub repo:

```
Source = "github.com/Ritesh/samplemodule"
```

Similarly, there are examples for consuming Terraform modules from other locations, and they are well documented at `https://www.terraform.io/docs/language/modules/sources.html#terraform-registry`.

Publishing a module involves pushing the code to a GitHub repo and then consuming them from other Terraform configurations using the `source` attribute, as shown earlier.

Nested Modules

Modules do not have a root configuration, and they need a root configuration to host the module and execute it. This does not mean that a module cannot contain modules themselves. Modules promote hierarchical authoring of resources. Root configuration relies on their immediate modules, and those modules themselves might rely on other modules. The modules can be nested multiple levels. There is no difference between a nested module and a parent module. They both are authored and consumed in the same way without any differences.

Module Best Practices

Modules are essentially Terraform scripts with a slight difference in authoring experience but a substantial difference in their usage. Some of the best practices that should be implemented are as follows:

- Modules should be published to a public repository if they are to be shared outside the team and should be published to a private repository if they will be shared within the organization.

- Modules should be shared from a repository like a Terraform repository or GitHub that provides good support from a security perspective.

- Modules should declare their dependence on a provider with regard to a specific version or a range of versions.

- Modules should bring together resources that are logically connected and share the same application lifecycle.

- Modules should be generic enough to be universally usable in the majority of cases. They should accept input variables and use them to be more generic and applied to the majority of cases.

- Modules should validate the input variables and declare both input and output variables as sensitive.

- Modules should not hard-code file paths or any string literal that would render a module less usable.

- Modules should output as much information using an output variable as will help other modules and root configuration to use them to configure other resources and modules. These outputs can help implement rich unit tests using tools like TerraTest.

Published modules should define their versions using the `semver(major:minor:patch)` notation. The minor version should be increased for any feature addition or improvement. The patch version should be increased for any small changes or bug fixes and major version for any breaking changes.

Summary

This chapter covered Terraform modules in more detail than previous chapters. Modules are one of the primary building blocks of Terraform, and having expertise in using them is needed to be a successful Terraform developer. Modules provide reusability, standardization, uniformity, and better manageability for Terraform configurations. Modules should be developed, tested, published before being consumed by Terraform root configurations. All these aspects were covered in detail within this chapter. Nested modules and module composition strategies were also covered. The next chapter will be focused on security and on writing Terraform scripts that manage sensitive data and secrets securely.

CHAPTER 6

Writing Secure Scripts with Terraform

Security is an important consideration for any enterprise application, and it is no different for infrastructure as code (IaC) and tools like Terraform. Terraform helps to provision infrastructure, which by default and design should be secure.

The design of the infrastructure is specific to a solution, and security should be considered as an important factor during its design. But there is more than just the infrastructure design. It is also important to take into consideration the process of delivering this infrastructure to different environments including production.

Enterprises use DevOps and implement continuous integration and continuous delivery pipelines to deliver both infrastructure and applications to environments. Terraform scripts are an important step within these CI/CD pipelines. Hence, security aspects for both Terraform scripts along with DevOps are crucial for the end-to-end security of the solution.

We will get into the details of the CI/CD pipeline in next Chapter. In this chapter, we will get into the details of Terraform security. Terraform has two different phases in its lifecycle.

- Design time
- Runtime

We will look at both of these stages from a security perspective and incorporate best practices to ensure that Terraform scripts can be authored and executed in a secure manner.

© Ritesh Modi 2021
R. Modi, *Deep-Dive Terraform on Azure*, https://doi.org/10.1007/978-1-4842-7328-9_6

Design-Time Considerations

Terraform scripts need to be authored in a way that is secure by default and that implements security best practices. These practices include the following:

- Avoiding hard-coding within scripts to use variables instead

- Using key vaults for storing and reading sensitive data

- Using the `sensitive` attribute for secret data so that it does not get displayed on the command line

- Storing state files securely in the remote back end with encryption enabled at rest as well during transmit

- Generating no outputs that contain sensitive information

- Using environment variables for supplying values to variables

- Removing the dependency on the `.tfvars` file

- Removing any authorized access to the state file

- Executing security scans using tools like TFscan to find insights about the Terraform scripts (the details of this will be covered in the subsequent chapter)

Runtime Considerations

When Terraform scripts are executed using the `terraform` command, it is referred to as the *runtime phase*. Security plays an important role here also. Security practices that should be used at runtime include the following:

- Authentication to Azure and the cloud provider. The secrets required for authentication should be supplied at runtime and not stored in files at design time.

- The secrets for authentication should be supplied using provider-specific environment variables, although there are multiple ways to supply values for variables.

- Information regarding remote storage account should be supplied at runtime rather than listed in Terraform files.

Terraform State File

Terraform state files can be easily opened using any text editor, and they contain both the outputs and the resource configuration. This means anyone who has access to the state file can easily read the resource configuration and output values. If a resource is configured with a secret or with sensitive information, it will be available in plain text in the state file. The state file is not encrypted, and the secrets are also not redacted.

A simple Terraform SQL server configuration accepts external values for the `administrator_login` and `administrator_login_password` attributes. The values are not hard-coded in HCL scripts.

```
resource "azurerm_sql_server" "book_sql_server" {
  name = var.sql_server_name

  location            = azurerm_resource_group.common_resource_group.location
  resource_group_name = azurerm_resource_group.common_resource_group.name

  version                      = "12.0"
  administrator_login          = var.sql_username_secret.value
  administrator_login_password = var.sql_password_secret.value

  tags = var.all_tags
}
```

The resultant state file resource section after successful execution of the Terraform script containing this resource declaration is shown here:

```
{
     "mode": "managed",
     "type": "azurerm_sql_server",
     "name": "book_sql_server",
     "provider": "provider[\"registry.terraform.io/hashicorp/azurerm\"]",
     "instances": [
       {
         "schema_version": 0,
         "attributes": {
           "administrator_login": "SqlServeradmin",
           "administrator_login_password": "SqlServer@1234 ",
           "connection_policy": "Default",
```

```
          "extended_auditing_policy": [],
        "fully_qualified_domain_name": "booktfsql1104.database.windows.net",
        "id": "/subscriptions/Xxx/resourceGroups/bookappresourcegroup/
             providers/Microsoft.Sql/servers/booktfsql1104",
        "identity": [],
        "location": "westeurope",
        "name": "booktfsql1104",
        "resource_group_name": "bookappresourcegroup",
        "tags": {
          "chapter": "terraform security",
          "owner": "ritesh"
        },
        "timeouts": null,
        "version": "12.0"
      },
      "sensitive_attributes": [],
      "private": "eyJlMmJmYjczMC1lY2FhLTExZTYtOGY4OC0zNDM2M2JjN2M0YzAi
        OnsiY3JlYXRlIjozNjAwMDAwMDAwMDAwLCJkZWxldGUiOjM2MDAwMDAwMDAwMDAs
        InJlYWQiOjMwMDAwMDAwMDAwMCwidXBkYXRlIjozNjAwMDAwMDAwMDAwfXO=",
    }
  ]
}
```

The lines in bold show that both the secrets (the administrator_login and administrator_login_password attributes) are visible as plain text in the state file.

This means the state files needs to be protected as a sensitive file. It should be accessible by a select few and from Terraform only. This file cannot be compromised and should be protected when stored at rest as well as during transmit.

Store the State File at a Remote Location

The Terraform state file can be stored in Azure blob storage within a container. The back-end configuration section in the HCL script lets Terraform know about the resource group, storage account, container name, name of state file, and keys to access the storage account. Storing the state file remotely helps not only in security, but also multiple developers can work on the same Terraform scripts and state. From a security perspective, it is much better to store the file remotely rather than on one developer's workstation.

Encrypt the State File at Rest

The Azure blob storage account is by default encrypted at rest. This ensures that anyone getting access to a storage account within Azure datacenter will not be able to retrieve comprehendible data stored in a state file. It is also possible to add a secondary encryption on top of the default one provided by Azure. For secondary encryption at rest, it is important to enable infrastructure encryption during the provisioning of a storage account. See Figure 6-1.

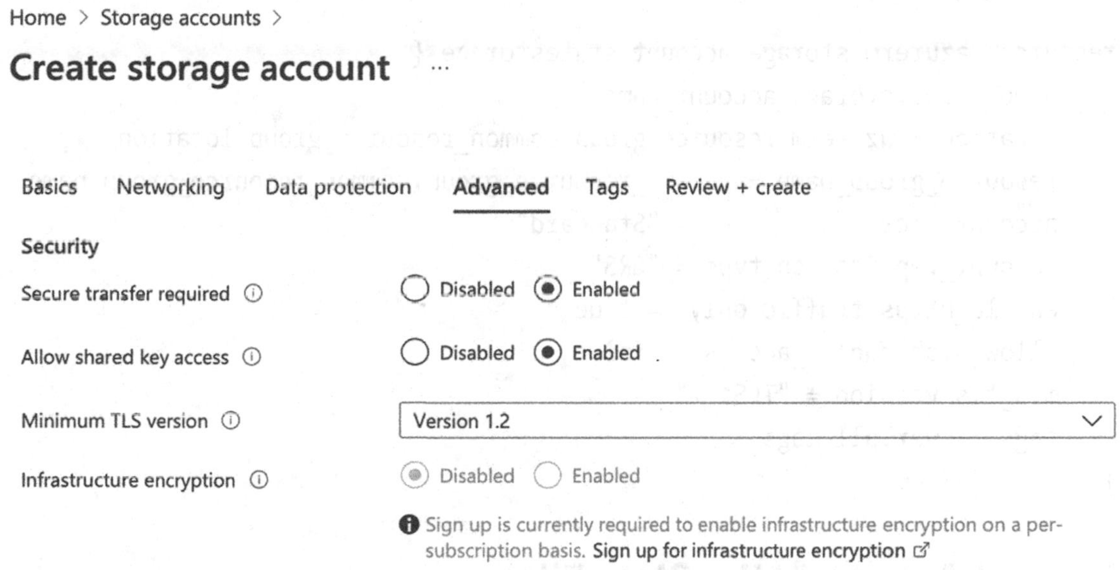

Home > Storage accounts >

Create storage account   ...

| Basics | Networking | Data protection | **Advanced** | Tags | Review + create |

Security

Secure transfer required ⓘ	⭕ Disabled ⦿ Enabled
Allow shared key access ⓘ	⭕ Disabled ⦿ Enabled .
Minimum TLS version ⓘ	Version 1.2 ⌄
Infrastructure encryption ⓘ	⦿ Disabled ⭕ Enabled

ⓘ Sign up is currently required to enable infrastructure encryption on a per-subscription basis. **Sign up for infrastructure encryption** ⌃

Figure 6-1. *Setting the Azure storage account minimum TLS version*

To enable infrastructure encryption, refer to `https://docs.microsoft.com/en-us/azure/storage/common/infrastructure-encryption-enable?tabs=azure-cli`. The link provides information about enabling and executing the commands using the Azure CLI related to infrastructure encryption, as shown next:

```
az feature register --namespace Microsoft.Storage \
    --name AllowRequireInfraStructureEncryption
```

```
az feature show --namespace Microsoft.Storage \
    --name AllowRequireInfraStructureEncryption

az provider register --namespace 'Microsoft.Storage'
```

State File Access Using SSL/TLS

Storing the state file encrypted at rest is part of a secure solution but not a complete solution. State files access and transfer over the wire should also be protected. For the secure transfer of a state file's data over the wire, it must use SSL/TLS during the transfer. This will ensure that the file content does not make much sense to eavesdroppers.

A storage account can be configured in Terraform as shown next. This ensures that all access happens over TLS/SSL.

```
resource  azurerm_storage_account statestorage {
    name = var.storage_account_name
    location = azurerm_resource_group.common_resource_group.location
    resource_group_name =azurerm_resource_group.common_resource_group.name
    account_tier            = "Standard"
    account_replication_type = "GRS"
    enable_https_traffic_only  = true
    allow_blob_public_access  = false
    min_tls_version = "TLS1_2"
    tags  = var.all_tags
}
```

Limited Access to the State File

The state file should not be accessible to the anonymous public users; only the administrator along with the Terraform execution account should be allowed to access it. It would defeat the entire purpose of securing the remote state file if it can be accessed easily by anyone.

Terraform Variables

Variables are one of the core Terraform element that helps in writing generic, reusable scripts. Variables allow us to reuse the same value in multiple places. It is quite easy to hard-code the values inline within Terraform scripts, but such scripts are not scalable and reusable. Other challenges with hard-coding are that these scripts are stored within version control system, and anyone having access to these systems could easily read all the confidential and sensitive information. So, hard-coding is not an acceptable practice. The alternative to hard-coding is to use variables.

There are multiple ways to pass values to variables in Terraform.

Using the .tfvars File

Values can be supplied to Terraform through `.tfvars` files. `"Terraform.tfvars"` is a special file that gets picked up automatically by Terraform, while other `.tfvars` files need to be specified using the `-var-file` command option.

Using the -var Option

The variable values can be supplied using the `-var` command option, as shown here:

```
Terraform apply -var='client_id=Xxx' -var='tenant_id=Xxx'
```

Using Environment Variables

Values for Terraform variables can be supplied using environment variables. Each variable defined within Terraform file can be supplied value using the `TF_VAR_*` pattern where * refers to a variable name. For example, if there is variable named `storage_account_name`, it can be supplied with a value using the `TF_VAR_storage_account_name` environment variable.

Provider-Specific Environment Variables

There are a few environment variables accepted by the Terraform provider without having corresponding variables within scripts. For example, `ARM_CLIENT_ID` is an environment variable that can be used to provide a value to the `client_id` attribute of the `azurerm` provider. Similarly, `ARM_TENANT_ID` is another environment variable that can be used to supply a value to the `tenant_id` attribute of the `azurerm` provider. If these environment variables exist within the execution context, they are used to auto assign to their corresponding provider related attribute. However, note that these environment variables are specific to the provider.

It is recommended that you use a hybrid approach for supplying values to variables. While non-sensitive values can be supplied using the .tfvars file, sensitive information should be supplied using a mix of environmental variables and TF_VAR environment variables.

When secrets are supplied using provider-specific environment variables, there is no way to use them as outputs or use them as variables within configuration, which also adds to additional security. However, their values will still be available in a state file.

Terraform Logs

Terraform generates log information for every execution. The level of detail in the logs can be set using the TF_LOG environment variable. Setting this environment variable to TRACE generates verbose detailed output, while setting it to ERROR generates log entries only for errors. The other possible values are DEBUG, INFO, and WARN.

It is also possible to generate a log file by setting the TF_LOG_FILE environment variable to the path of the log file. This will redirect all log entries to the file mentioned in this environment variable.

It is not an ideal configuration to generate log files during the normal course of execution. These log files should be used only for debugging purposes. In fact, they should be avoided and should not be used in a production environment at all. Even if these log files with TRACE details are generated, they should be protected just like state files since they can contain sensitive and secret information, so all rules related to securing a Terraform state file are also applicable to the log files.

Terraform CLI

All Terraform scripts are executed using the Terraform CLI commands. These commands generate messages and they are sent to log files or to standard output device. The output does not differentiate between sensitive and non-sensitive data. All resource processing and output values are visible as plain text within the logs.

It is not ideal to write sensitive information to logs. Terraform offers 'sensitive' attribute for outputs and variables from version 0.14.0 onward. Using the sensitive attribute along with Boolean true/false decides whether the information should be redacted or displayed. It is to be noted that the sensitive attribute does redaction only for output on the screen. These values are still available as plain text within the log and state files. It is also possible to redirect the values to an external source or a text file in plain text format.

Secure Terraform Script Authoring

We'll now focus on the secure Terraform script authoring practices for the Azure cloud. Terraform scripts provision resources and they at times need sensitive data to configure the resources. This sensitive information should ideally be stored in Azure Key Vault. There are various multiple approaches to use a Key Vault from an organization's perspective. For example, an Organization would like to put all secrets and sensitive information in a centralized Key Vault for an engagement comprising of multiple projects. Similarly, it is quite possible to have a unique Key Vault for each project within an engagement. Further again it is possible to for each environment in a project to have its own Key Vault. In all these cases, secrets should be provisioned and consumed. The provisioning of secrets and access management is generally done by administrator while other consume them. In this chapter, Key Vault is viewed from a project perspective with an identified administrator. It means there is a common Key Vault across all environments (dev, test, prod) in a project. It does not mean other practices are not valid. They are equally good in design and applicable and can be applied depending on requirements. If you have understood the usage of Key Vault in given scenario, it can easily be used in other approaches. There are two distinct set of activities performed each by administrator and application/solutions team.

- *Admin*: Provisions security resources and secrets.

- *Solutions team*: Consumes security resources and secrets. The Azure DevOps account is also part of this group.

In this section, we will go through the entire lifecycle of both admin and solutions team to provision resources using secure practices with Terraform. You should use the code from the book's source code repository for this chapter and while doing so ensure that the values of the variables are modified according to your environment.

Admin Activities

An administrator has full access to Azure subscription and its resources. In Azure terms, the administrator is the owner and has all permissions on all the resources. Solutions team generally have contributor and reader permissions. They cannot provision security-related resources and configurations.

Storing Secrets

It all starts when the administrator provisions the critical infrastructure and secrets needed by other projects and solutions.

The administrator should provision a new service principal within Azure AD through the portal or automation(az cli, az PowerShell, etc.). This service principal is created outside of Terraform and is used to execute admin related Terraform scripts. The administrator for example then use Az cli using the service principal for authenticating to Azure prior to executing Terraform scripts. This is also known as az cli authentication method in Terraform.

The admin script starts with the provisioning of a resource group that will contain Azure Key Vault for storing sensitive data and a storage account for storing remote Terraform state files. The code for resource group is shown next:

```
resource azurerm_resource_group common_resource_group {
    name = var.resource_group_name
    location = var.resource_group_location

    tags = var.all_tags
}
```

The scripts should provision a storage account with a container and generate an associated SAS token. This token would be handed over to solutions team and this will allow them to securely store their state file in this storage account.

The script to create a storage account and container is shown next:

```
resource  azurerm_storage_account statestorage {
    name = var.storage_account_name
    location = azurerm_resource_group.common_resource_group.location
    resource_group_name =azurerm_resource_group.common_resource_group.name
    account_tier            =   "Standard"
```

```
    account_replication_type =    "GRS"
    enable_https_traffic_only  = true
    allow_blob_public_access  =  false
    min_tls_version = "TLS1_2"
    tags  = var.all_tags
}

resource azurerm_storage_container statecontainer {
  name                    = var.container_name
  storage_account_name  = azurerm_storage_account.statestorage.name
  container_access_type = "private"
}
```

Notice that the storage account can be accessed using HTTPS protocol only and does not allow public access; this means to access the storage, an account key or a SAS token, or role-based access control should be used.

Once the storage account is provisioned, it can be used to generate the SAS token. A Terraform Data Resource is used to generate the SAS token, as shown next:

```
data azurerm_storage_account_sas state_container_sas_token {
  connection_string = azurerm_storage_account.statestorage.primary_
                      connection_string
  https_only        = true
  signed_version    = "2017-07-29"

  resource_types {
    service   = true
    container = true
    object    = true
  }

  services {
    blob  = true
    queue = false
    table = false
    file  = false
  }
```

```
  start  = "2021-03-21T00:00:00Z"
  expiry = "2021-09-21T00:00:00Z"

  permissions {
    read    = true
    write   = true
    delete  = true
    list    = true
    add     = true
    create  = true
    update  = true
    process = true
  }
}
```

Notice that the start and expiry time should be configured based on the project's secret expiration policy. Similarly, to store the state file as a blob within a container and enable access from Terraform, permissions should be configured while generating SAS Tokens. There should be permissions enabled such that Terraform can effectively add, delete, update, and read the state files.

Next, the Terraform script should create a new service application and principal either using a password or certificate credential. This service principal is provisioned for other teams to use it and execute their project specific Terraform scripts. The script for provisioning a new service application, service principal, and associated password is shown next:

```
resource "azuread_application" "book_service_application" {
  display_name              = var.ad_application_name
  available_to_other_tenants = false
  oauth2_allow_implicit_flow = true
  owners                    = [data.azurerm_client_config.primary.object_id]
}

resource "azuread_service_principal" "book_service_principle" {
  application_id                  = azuread_application.book_service_
                                    application.application_id
```

```
  app_role_assignment_required = false

}

resource "azuread_service_principal_password" "book_service_principle_
password" {
  service_principal_id = azuread_service_principal.book_service_principle.id
  description          = "My managed password"
  value                = var.ad_application_password
  end_date             = "2099-01-01T01:02:03Z"
}
```

The newly created service principal will eventually be handed over to the solutions team and it would be used for provisioning resources on Azure. This Service Principal should at least be granted "Contribute" permissions on Azure subscription or a resource group. The script for providing the "Contribute" permission to service principal at the subscription level is shown next:

```
resource "azurerm_role_assignment" "executor" {
  scope                = data.azurerm_subscription.primary.id
  role_definition_name = "Contributor"
  principal_id         = data.azurerm_client_config.primary.object_id
}
resource "azurerm_role_assignment" "book-service-principle-role" {
  scope                = data.azurerm_subscription.primary.id
  role_definition_name = "Contributor"
  principal_id         = azuread_service_principal.book_service_principle.
                         object_id
}
```

Next, a key vault should be provisioned for storing all the secrets needed by other applications and solutions. This typically includes secrets and sensitive information like connection strings, user names, passwords, URIs, URLs, tokens, and any other data deemed to be sensitive in nature. The script for provisioning a key vault is shown next:

```
resource "azurerm_key_vault" "book_keyvault" {
```

```
name = var.keyvault_name

location                = azurerm_resource_group.common_resource_group.location
resource_group_name = azurerm_resource_group.common_resource_group.name

tenant_id = data.azurerm_client_config.primary.tenant_id

sku_name = "standard"

enabled_for_deployment          = true
enabled_for_disk_encryption     = true
enabled_for_template_deployment = true
purge_protection_enabled        = true

tags = var.all_tags
}
```

The key vault should be accessible by the newly created service principal alongside the existing used service principal. The script for providing service principal access to the key vault is shown next and is done using the AzureRM `azurerm_key_vault_access_policy` resource. There are two sets of sensitive data in our case: keys and secrets. Each of them can be configured for different levels of permissions for the service principal. The `depends_on` attribute ensures that a key vault is provisioned only after the service principal has already been provisioned. Both the service principals (one that is newly created within the current configuration and another that is used for executing the Terraform scripts) are concatenated into a single list within the `locals` block and assigned to the `keyvault_policy_owners` variable. This local variable is further used while provisioning key vault policies. For each service principal, a new policy is created in a loop using the `count` meta attribute.

```
data "azurerm_subscription" "primary" {
}

data "azurerm_client_config" "primary" {
}

locals {
  keyvault_policy_owners = concat([azuread_service_principal.book_service_
principle.object_id], [data.azurerm_client_config.primary.object_id])
}
```

```
resource "azurerm_key_vault_access_policy" "book_owner_access_policy" {
  count = length(local.keyvault_policy_owners )

  object_id    = local.keyvault_policy_owners["${count.index}"]
  tenant_id    = data.azurerm_client_config.primary.tenant_id
  key_vault_id = azurerm_key_vault.book_keyvault.id

  key_permissions = [
    "Backup",
    "Create",
    "Decrypt",
    "Delete",
    "Encrypt",
    "Get",
    "Import",
    "List",
    "Purge",
    "Recover",
    "Restore",
    "Sign",
    "UnwrapKey",
    "Update",
    "Verify",
    "WrapKey",
  ]

  secret_permissions = [
    "Backup",
    "Delete",
    "Get",
    "List",
    "Purge",
    "Recover",
    "Restore",
    "Set",
  ]
```

```
  depends_on = [
    azurerm_role_assignment.book-service-principle-role,
    azuread_service_principal_password.book_service_principle_password,
    azuread_service_principal.book_service_principle
  ]

}
```

Notice that `tenant_id` is not supplied as a variable to the `tenant_id` attribute of the access policy resource. Instead, it is obtained from the data source of type `azurerm_client_config`. This resource provides information such as `client_id`, `tenant_id`, and `subscription_id` related to the service principal used for authenticating to Azure. Using this approach helps in removing the dependency on variables that are holding secrets related to authentication and tenant information.

Finally, the script provision secrets in Azure Key Vault using the `azurerm_key_vault_secret` resource. The values for the name of the secret and its associated value are obtained from a map variable, which are supplied at runtime during Terraform command execution. These secrets should be not part of the `.tfvars` file under any circumstances. The `map` variable is looped using the `for_each` loop, and for each name-value pair a new secret is generated in Azure Key Vault. `depends_on` ensures that a secret is not created before the key vault is provisioned.

```
resource "azurerm_key_vault_secret" "sql-username" {
  for_each = var.keyvault_pairs

  name         = each.key
  value        = each.value
  key_vault_id = azurerm_key_vault.book_keyvault.id

    depends_on = [
    azurerm_key_vault_access_policy.book_owner_access_policy
  ]
}
```

Executing Terraform Admin Script

After authoring the script used by the administrator to provision resources that are crucial for storing secrets and other sensitive information for other applications, it's time to provision them by executing Terraform's `init`, `plan`, and `apply` commands.

As you know by now, there are multiple ways to supply values for variables declared within Terraform scripts. It is safer to use provider-specific environment variables for sensitive data like `client_id` and `subscription_id` since they are read automatically by the provider and there is no explicit reference to them within the script.

The `azurerm` provider utilizes a few environment variables if they are set explicitly before execution. These environment variables are generally related to sensitive data and used for authenticating to Azure. `ARM_SUBSCRIPTION_ID`, `ARM_CLIENT_ID`, `ARM_CLIENT_SECRET`, and `ARM_TENANT_ID` environment variables are assigned appropriate values and exported using Bash's export command. The `export` command is used on Linux- and Mac-based systems.

```
export ARM_SUBSCRIPTION_ID=Xxx

export ARM_CLIENT_ID=Xxx

export ARM_CLIENT_SECRET=Xxx

export ARM_TENANT_ID=xxx
```

In the case of the Windows operating system, PowerShell's $env variable can be used to add new environment variables, as shown next:

```
$env:ARM_SUBSCRIPTION_ID=Xxx
```

The provider configuration within the script should not use any attributes related to authentication when using this approach, as shown next:

```
provider "azurerm" {
  features {}
}

provider "azuread" {

}
```

The next step is to initialize the Terraform environment by downloading the modules and provider if not already downloaded using the init command, as shown next:

```
Terraform init
```

After initialization, the plan command is executed along with variables required for the Terraform script to execute. It is also possible to supply values for all variables using environment variables. These environment variables start with the TF_VAR_ prefix along with the name of the actual variable. Notice that our configuration declares a variable called resource_group_name. The value for this variable can be supplied using an environment variable called TF_VAR_resource_group_name. If we want, we can supply all variables values needed by the Terraform configuration in this way. These environment variables can be provisioned and scoped at the command level or scoped at session level. The environment variables shown next are scoped at the command level, and they are not available once the command completes its execution:

```
TF_VAR_resource_group_name=bookrg-terraform TF_VAR_resource_group_
location="west europe" TF_VAR_all_tags='{"owner":"ritesh", "environment":"dev"}'
TF_VAR_storage_account_name=bookrgterraform1004 TF_VAR_container_
name=terraformstaterepo TF_VAR_keyvault_name=bookky-terraform TF_VAR_keyvault_
pairs='{"sqlusername":"someusernamr","sqlpassword":"somepassword"}' TF_VAR_ad_
application_name=book_app_name TF_VAR_ad_application_password=dfqe&*^sss123
terraform plan
```

After the plan command succeeds, the terraform apply command can be executed with the same set of variable values as used during the plan command.

```
TF_VAR_resource_group_name=bookrg-terraform TF_VAR_resource_group_
location="west europe" TF_VAR_all_tags='{"owner":"ritesh", "environment":"dev"}'
TF_VAR_storage_account_name=bookrgterraform1004 TF_VAR_container_
name=terraformstaterepo TF_VAR_keyvault_name=bookky-terraform TF_VAR_keyvault_
pairs='{"sqlusername":"someusername","sqlpassword":"somepassword"}' TF_VAR_ad_
application_name=book_app_name TF_VAR_ad_application_password=dfqe&*^sss123
terraform apply -auto-approve
```

After the apply command completes successfully, there should be a storage account and a key vault with a couple of secrets provisioned, all within a resource group that are ready to be utilized by other applications, solutions, and projects.

```
azurerm_key_vault_secret.sql-username["sqlpassword"]: Creating...
azurerm_key_vault_secret.sql-username["sqlusername"]: Creating...
azurerm_key_vault_secret.sql-username["sqlpassword"]: Creation complete after 5s |
azurerm_key_vault_secret.sql-username["sqlusername"]: Creation complete after 6s |

Apply complete! Resources: 5 added, 0 changed, 0 destroyed.

Outputs:

objectsids = <sensitive>
sas_token = <sensitive>
sp_auth = <sensitive>
sp_data = <sensitive>
subscription_data = <sensitive>
```

Utilizing Secrets for Remote State

This section relates to building infrastructure for solutions and applications that depend on secrets and sensitive data provisioned using previous scripts by the administrator.

The administrator has already provisioned a storage account and its associated container and generated a SAS token. The administrator would eventually hand over these details to the application team. The application team authoring Terraform scripts for their own solution should use the storage details to store their state file on the remote back end. The configuration to store the state file in the Azure storage remote back end is shown next:

```
terraform {
  required_providers {
    azurerm = {
      source  = "hashicorp/azurerm"
      version = "=2.53.0"
    }
  }

  backend "azurerm" {
    resource_group_name    = "Xxx"
    storage_account_name   = "xxx"
    container_name         = "xxx"
    key                    = "xxx"
    sas_token              = "xxx"
  }
}
```

Notice that the backend element within the `terraform` block. This block is executed even before the Terraform variables are initialized, so the variables cannot be used to configure the storage account details in the script.

The way to provide dynamic values to the remote backend without any hard-coding is to use the `backend-config` command options available with the `terraform init` command.

`terraform init` provides a `backend-config` option, and they can accept name-value pairs, with each one related to an attribute in the back-end configuration. The same is shown in the next command:

```
terraform init -backend-config='resource_group_name=bookrg-
terraform' -backend-config='storage_account_name=bookrgterraform1004'
-backend-config='container_name=terraformstaterepo' -backend-
config='key=bookterraformstate.tfstate' -backend-config='sas_token=Xxx'
```

Notice that there are multiple backend-config options used, one for each attribute, and each option contains a name-value pair with the attribute name and its associated value.

The previous script authenticated to Azure using a service principal, and the provider was not configured explicitly with attributes related to the service principal; rather, it used the provider-specific environment variables to supply service principal values (using the `export` command in bash) and then initialized the provider. The provider checked for the presence of these environment variable and utilized them to authenticate to Azure.

An alternate to using a provider-specific environment variable is to use variables directly. In this approach, the variables are used directly in scripts, as shown here:

```
provider "azurerm" {
  subscription_id = var.subscription_id
  tenant_id       = var.tenant_id
  client_id       = var.client_id
  features {}
}
```

The `subscription_id` attribute is a supplied value from the `subscription_id` variable, and the value for this variable can be supplied using the `-var` command option. It is not a good idea to use the `.tfvars` file to store secrets and sensitive information.

Notice that the `client_secret` attribute is missing from the set of attributes available in the provider configuration, and this is on purpose. The client secret can be supplied using a provider-specific environment variable, while others can get a value from the `-var` command option. This is also known as a *hybrid approach.* The `client_secret` environment variable should be available (using the `export` command) prior to running the `terraform init` command.

```
export ARM_CLIENT_SECRET=Xxx
```

The `plan` command can be supplied with the command scope environment variable using the TF_VAR approach shown next. Note that the values for `administrator_login` and `administrator_login_password` are strings that correspond to the names of secrets in the vault.

```
TF_VAR_resource_group_name=bookrg-terraform TF_VAR_resource_
group_location="west europe" TF_VAR_all_tags='{"owner":"ritesh",
"environment":"dev"}' TF_VAR_administrator_login=sqlusername TF_VAR_
administrator_login_password=sqlpassword TF_VAR_keyvault_name=bookky-
terraform TF_VAR_keyvault_pairs='{"sqlusername":"Xxx","sqlpassword":"Xxx"}'
terraform plan
```

These variables can also be supplied values using the `-var` option, as shown next:

```
terraform plan -var='administrator_login=sqlusername' -var='administrator_
login_password=sqlpassword' -var=' keyvault_name=bookky-terraform' -var=
'keyvault_pairs='{"sqlusername":"Citynextadmin","sqlpassword":"Cityne
xt!1233"}'
```

Other nonsensitive data can be supplied using the `terraform.tfvars` file, as shown next:

```
resource_group_name  = "bookappresourcegroup"
 resource_group_location  = "west europe"
 all_tags  = {
    "owner": "ritesh",
    "chapter" : "terraform security"
}
sql_server_name  = "booktfsql1104"
allowed_cidr_list = ["0.0.0.0/32"]
```

The apply command is similar to the plan command and is shown here:

```
TF_VAR_resource_group_name=bookrg-terraform TF_VAR_resource_
group_location="west europe" TF_VAR_all_tags='{"owner":"ritesh",
"environment":"dev"}' TF_VAR_administrator_login=sqlusername TF_VAR_
administrator_login_password=sqlpassword TF_VAR_keyvault_name=bookky-
terraform TF_VAR_keyvault_pairs='{"sqlusername":"someusername","sqlpassword
":"somepassword"}' terraform apply -auto-approve
```

Utilizing Secrets in Applications

The application infrastructure provisions a resource group along with Azure SQL Server
and its associated firewall rules for showcasing the following:

- The usage of secrets using Azure Key Vault

- Environment variables

- Remote storage

- Passing nonsensitive information using terraform.tfvars

- Supplying a few variables using the -var command option

Since the SQL Server resource is dependent on secrets from Azure Key Vault, it is
necessary to declare data resources in the configuration related to Azure Key Vault and
secrets, as shown here:

```
data "azurerm_key_vault" "bookkeyvault" {
  name                = var.key_vault_name
  resource_group_name = var.key_vault_rg
}

data "azurerm_key_vault_secret" "sql_username_secret" {
  name         = var.administrator_login
  key_vault_id = data.azurerm_key_vault.bookkeyvault.id
}

data "azurerm_key_vault_secret" "sql_password_secret" {
  name         = var.administrator_password
  key_vault_id = data.azurerm_key_vault.bookkeyvault.id
}
```

Notice that the key vault name and `administrator_login` and `administrator_login_password` are variable dependent, and these variables are supplied at runtime using `-vars` command option or environmental variables.

Next, a resource group is provisioned, and all of its attributes get values from variables, as shown next:

```
resource azurerm_resource_group common_resource_group {
    name = var.resource_group_name
    location = var.resource_group_location

    tags = var.all_tags
}
```

The next resource declaration is `azurerm_sql_server`, and it is dependent on the resource group; so, an implicit dependency is defined using the `location` and `resource_group_name` attributes. These attributes refer to the resource group resource using the resource group resource type, name, and its specific property. The `resource` attributes related to the login and password also get their values in a similar way, with the difference being that they refer to data sources that return the secret values from Azure Key Vault.

```
resource "azurerm_sql_server" "book_sql_server" {
  name = var.sql_server_name

  location              = azurerm_resource_group.common_resource_group.location
  resource_group_name = azurerm_resource_group.common_resource_group.name

  version               = "12.0"
  administrator_login            = data.azurerm_key_vault_secret.sql_
                                   username_secret.value
  administrator_login_password = data.azurerm_key_vault_secret.sql_
                                   password_secret.value

  tags = var.all_tags
}

resource "azurerm_sql_firewall_rule" "book_sql_firewall_rule" {
  count = length(var.allowed_cidr_list)

  name                = "firewall-rule-${count.index}"
```

```
resource_group_name = azurerm_resource_group.common_resource_group.name
server_name          = azurerm_sql_server.book_sql_server.name

start_ip_address = cidrhost(var.allowed_cidr_list[count.index], 0)
end_ip_address   = cidrhost(var.allowed_cidr_list[count.index], -1)
}
```

Notice that there is no mention of any secret in the script related to the username and password. Neither of these values is obtained from variables; instead, they are fetched from Azure Key Vault and fed directly to the resource configuration.

Summary

This chapter explored security issues while using Terraform as configuration management tool for infrastructure. Security is one of the key aspects for any solution, and the infrastructure plays a vital part in the overall security for the solution. The infrastructure provisioned should be secure by default, but the process of delivering that infrastructure is equally important, and that is where security in Terraform starts to matter. Terraform provides state files that are easy to read as they can be opened in any text editor. They contain all the information including sensitive data, so they must be protected. They should be stored in remote storage with encryption at rest and secure transmission enabled. They should be accessible by only a few authorized people. The variables concept in Terraform helps in supplying sensitive data at runtime during execution, and there are multiple ways to supply values for variables, including environment variables. Using provider-specific environment variables is a preferred means of suppling values to sensitive variables, wherever possible. Finally, using a vault service to store the secrets and having authorized identities reading them is way to implement security with Terraform and IaC in general. In the next chapter, we will go into writing CI/CD pipelines for Terraform scripts and validating them before using them for deployment.

CHAPTER 7

CI/CD with Terraform

Terraform helps in implementing Infrastructure as Code (IaC), and this code should reside alongside the application code in the same version control repository. The Terraform code is written and managed by multiple developers who need to collaborate and integrate their code on an ongoing basis. It is important that a version control repository is established for teams working on Terraform and appropriate processes are incorporated to validate, verify, and merge the code. The Terraform state should also be stored remotely to enable collaboration between multiple developers.

The Terraform code should undergo the process of validation and checks for compliance like any application code would go through. The application lifecycle is also applicable for Terraform code. However, the tools used to implement the application lifecycle and validation are different than the ones used for IaC-based tools like Terraform.

A separate build and release process (continuous integration/continuous deployment) should be implemented, with each having activities and steps that are responsible for carrying out compliance checks, security checks, validation, tests, etc. to ensure that the code submitted by developers meets the policies, requirements, and standards laid down by the project and organization.

The build pipelines should execute as soon as changes are submitted by developers, and only after the successful execution of the build pipelines should the code be merged with higher-order branches.

This chapter focuses on the CI/CD pipelines for Terraform-related code. The chapter will introduce a sample Terraform project consisting of Terraform scripts, Terraform modules, Golang-based unit and integration tests, the configuration for the Terraform linter, and more. There are preparation steps that should be executed prior to implementing the build and release pipelines. These steps will be enumerated, and then we'll go over the process of implementing pipelines for Terraform scripts; build as well as deployment (release) will be covered in this chapter. There are multiple different ways to organize and structure Terraform scripts for the purpose of executing them from pipelines. I am mentioning couple of these different ways to organize the code, and

© Ritesh Modi 2021
R. Modi, *Deep-Dive Terraform on Azure*, https://doi.org/10.1007/978-1-4842-7328-9_7

the pipeline code should be written to ensure it can read the files in the given structure. One way to organize the code is to have completely different self-contained folders containing all Terraform files for each environment. One of the issues with this approach is that it introduces Terraform code duplication. Another way is to have code common across environments and just have different configuration for variables. The second approach is used in this chapter. Again, there are multiple approaches to generate Terraform plan and apply them. It could be that plan files are generated once during build process for each environment and published as artifacts. When deployment stages are initiated, they would retrieve their own specific plan file and apply it. This ensures that anytime the code changes happen, it passes through the build stage otherwise the new plan is not generated. On the other hand, another approach is that each deployment stage can generated a plan file based on current code and used it to apply the Terraform configuration. There is possibility of different code coming from different Git branches generating different plans and applied in different environment. In this approach, there is possibility of drifts between the environments. The first approach of generating Terraform plan files for all environments is used in this chapter. It is to be noted that each of these approaches have their pros and cons and each must be evaluated for the current project in hand.

Creating the Sample Terraform Project

In this part of the chapter, we will go through a Terraform project (the source code is available with the book's code) and use it in CI/CD pipeline. The project has a top-level folder named `TerraformEngineering` with `environments`, `modules`, and `tests` as subfolders. The Terraform code provisions a resource group and a storage account. The resource group will be implemented as a Terraform module and the storage account as a Terraform resource. Although the Terraform code is simple with just a couple of resources and a module, it illustrates all the flavors of Terraform scripting and engineering practices when implementing a successful Terraform-based CI/CD pipeline. A brief summary of folder structure is mentioned next:

- *environments*: This holds the main Terraform files that will be executed to create the `dev`, `test`, and `production` environments. The same files will be executed for all the environments; however, the parameters will change from environment to environment based on `.tfvars` file.

- *varvalues*: This folder contains the variables file responsible for declaring and supplying parameters to each environment. It contains one Terraform variables file for each environment.

- *modules*: This folder contains reusable code in the form of Terraform modules. It has a single module to provision the Azure resource group.

- *tests*: This folder contains unit and integration tests for the Terraform code in the modules and environments folder. It also contains the `fixtures` folder.

- *fixtures*: This folder contains the Terraform HCL scripts using the Terraform modules. Terraform modules cannot be directly executed. They should be declared within a Terraform script that can be used along with the Terraform CLI. The `fixtures` folder is meant to define the Terraform script with the sole aim to utilize modules. In our case, it's a resource group module. The unit tests for the module will use the code in fixtures to test the modules. Think of this folder as a parent Terraform script for resource group module to enable unit tests. See Figure 7-1.

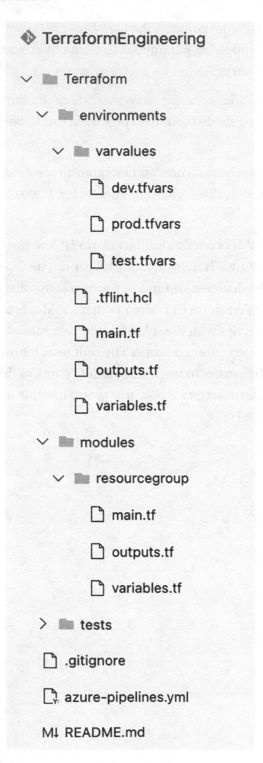

Figure 7-1. *Project folder and file organization*

We need a version control repository for storing code and enable collaboration between multiple developers. Azure DevOps is a great platform for storing code files, versioning, utilizing Git repositories, and implementing CI/CD pipelines (build and release pipelines).

A new Git-based Azure DevOps project within an existing or new organization should be created to implement the solution shown in this chapter. By default, a single repository with a single main branch is created. There could be multiple branches for a solution and pull requests should be used to merge code from one branch to another. Figure 7-2 shows that develop branch is already created from Main branch.

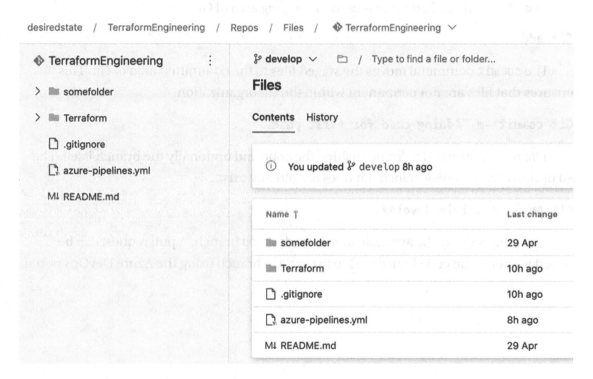

Figure 7-2. *Git-based Azure DevOps repo with project files and folder checked in*

The next set of steps shows the way to collaborate and work with version controlled Terraform files. The files stored in version controlled repository should be cloned to local machine, carve out a new branch out from it, add and modify the scripts and eventually pushing the new branch to the repository. The way to bring changes in other branches is to create a pull request consisting of your changes.

The clone command copies all the branches and code there-in to the local workstation. This activity might need authentication. This will copy the main branch and designate it as a default current branch.

Git clone "<<URL of the repository>>"

The checkout command will create a new develop branch and will also make it the current branch. The -b option helps in creating a new branch with the name develop.

Git checkout -b develop

The add command adds the files to the staging area of Git.

Git add .

The commit command moves the staged files to the committed area of Git. This ensures that files are not permanent within the Git organization.

Git commit -m "Adding code for first push"

The push command helps in pushing the code and optionally the branch itself. The -u option creates a new branch if it does not already exist.

Git push -u origin develop

Now, the code will be available in remote develop branch. A pull request can be raised to merge the code from develop to the main branch using the Azure DevOps portal.

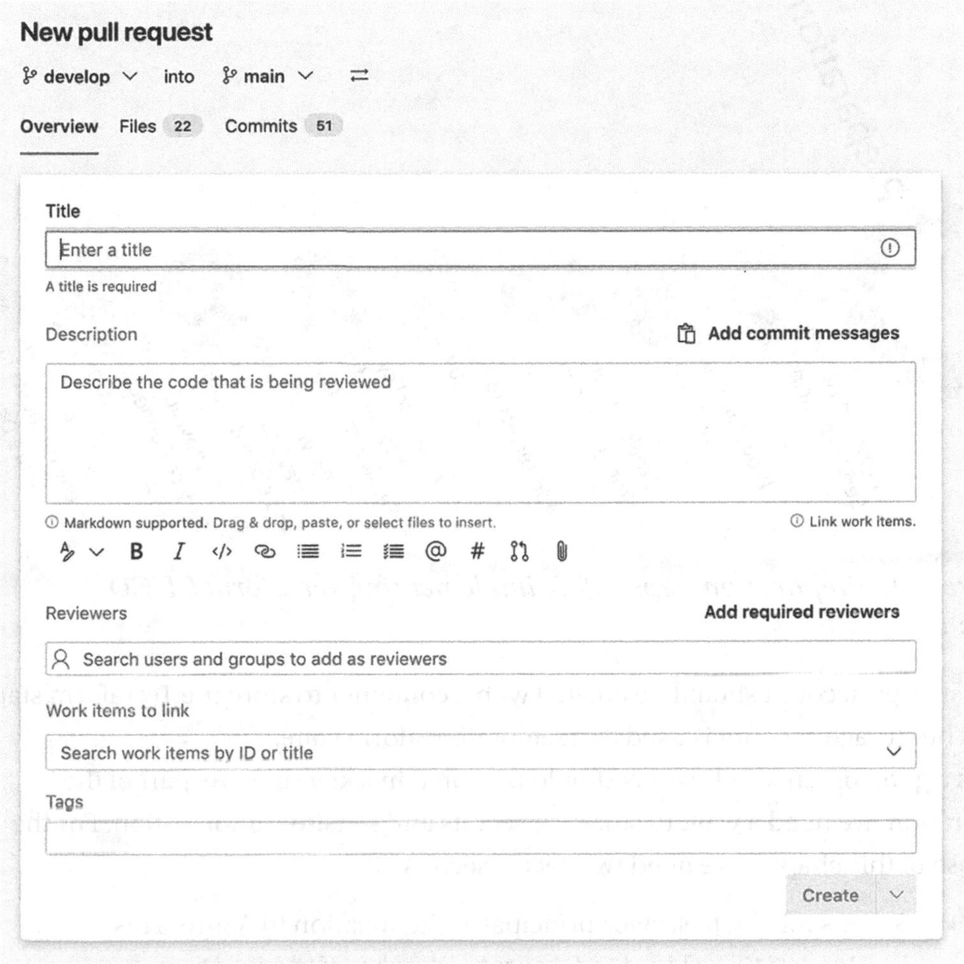

Figure 7-3. *Pull request form in Azure DevOps*

Preparation

There are a few steps as part of the preparation that should be executed before we can execute the Terraform scripts. These preparation steps should ideally be automated.

Figure 7-4 shows the activities that are part of the preparation steps.

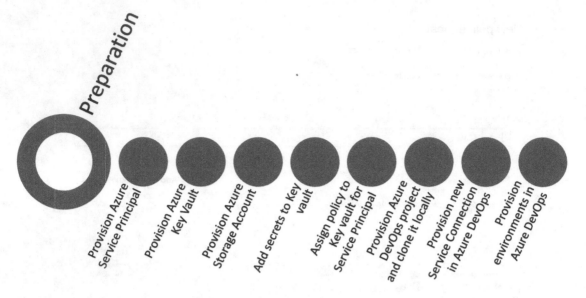

Figure 7-4. *Preparation steps before implementing Terraform CI/CD pipelines*

A storage account should be created with a container to store the Terraform state files. The storage account is used as a remote Terraform state.

As a good practice, all secrets should be stored in a key vault. As part of the preparation, we need a vault to store our secrets and sensitive information. For the purpose of this chapter, we need two sets of secrets.

- Secrets related to service principal authentication to Azure. This involves storing `client_id`, `tenant_id`, `subscription_id`, and `client_secret` in a key vault.

- Information related to storing the Terraform state file in remote Azure blob storage. This involves storing the storage account name, the resource group of the storage account, the container name within the storage account, the name of the state file, and the access token related to the storage account.

The steps to create a storage account and key vault are not shown here as they have already been covered in previous chapter on security. The key vault should contain secrets needed by the pipeline and terraform scripts. See Figure 7-5.

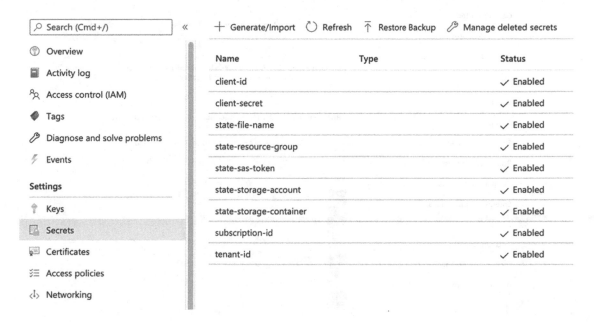

Figure 7-5. Azure Key Vault with secrets

A service principal with secret credentials should also be created for authentication purposes from both Azure DevOps and Terraform in Azure Active Directory.

App registration aids in the provisioning of a service principal. See Figure 7-6.

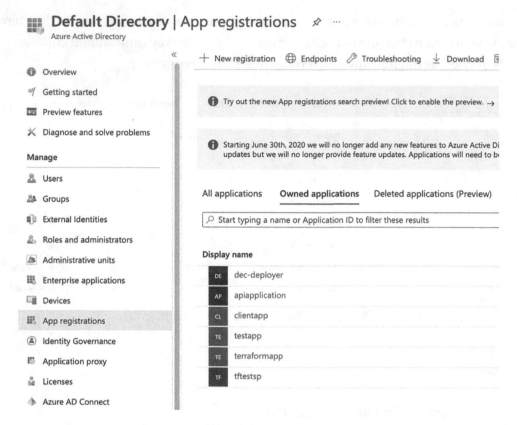

Figure 7-6. *Service principal creation using app registrations*

It is also important to add an access policy in our key vault for the newly created service principal and assign appropriate permissions to it. See Figure 7-7.

+ Add Access Policy

Current Access Policies

	Name	Email	Key Permissions		Secret Permissions		Certificate Permissio...		Action
APPLICATION									
	tftestsp		16 selected	∨	8 selected	∨	16 selected	∨	Delete
	terraformapp		16 selected	∨	8 selected	∨	16 selected	∨	Delete
	testapp		2 selected	∨	2 selected	∨	2 selected	∨	Delete

Figure 7-7. *Key vault access policy for the service principal*

Another step that should be undertaken is to provision environments within Azure DevOps. These environments will be used in deployment stages within the YAML pipelines. The environments do not have any resources or configuration. They have manual approval enabled with the administrator email address. This will ensure that any deployment stage before its execution will need an approval from appropriate authority. Three environments, namely, `dev`, `test` and `prod`, are created. They will be utilized within YAML pipelines later as targets and Terraform scripts would execute against each of them one after another. See Figure 7-8.

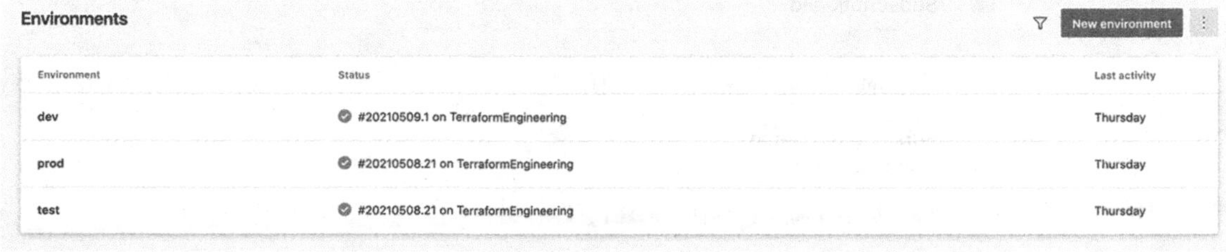

Environment	Status	Last activity
Environments		New environment
dev	✓ #20210509.1 on TerraformEngineering	Thursday
prod	✓ #20210508.21 on TerraformEngineering	Thursday
test	✓ #20210508.21 on TerraformEngineering	Thursday

Figure 7-8. *Provisioned multiple environments in Azure DevOps*

One last action that should be taken is to create a service connection in Azure DevOps within our organization based on the Azure Resource Group Manual Service Principal option. It requires the service principal ID (a.k.a. client ID), client secret, Azure subscription name, subscription ID, and tenant ID. The verify action should show success for successful connectivity to Azure from Azure DevOps. See Figure 7-9.

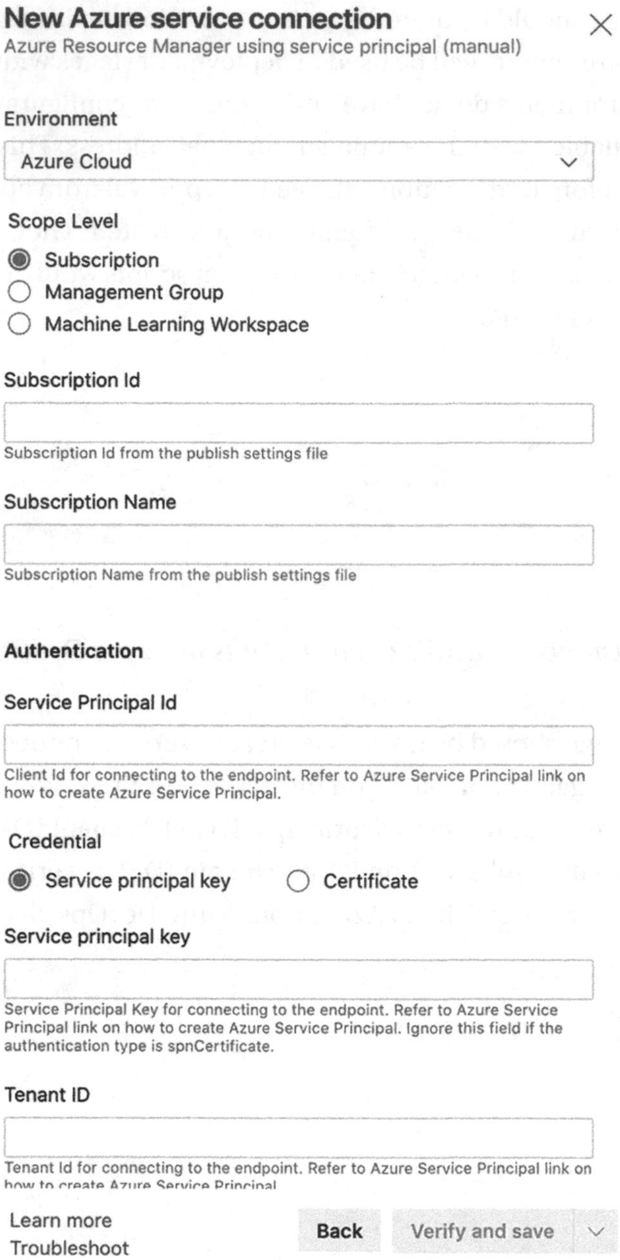

New Azure service connection   ✕
Azure Resource Manager using service principal (manual)

Environment

| Azure Cloud   ∨ |

Scope Level

◉ Subscription
◯ Management Group
◯ Machine Learning Workspace

Subscription Id

| |

Subscription Id from the publish settings file

Subscription Name

| |

Subscription Name from the publish settings file

Authentication

Service Principal Id

| |

Client Id for connecting to the endpoint. Refer to Azure Service Principal link on
how to create Azure Service Principal.

Credential

◉ Service principal key   ◯ Certificate

Service principal key

| |

Service Principal Key for connecting to the endpoint. Refer to Azure Service
Principal link on how to create Azure Service Principal. Ignore this field if the
authentication type is spnCertificate.

Tenant ID

| |

Tenant Id for connecting to the endpoint. Refer to Azure Service Principal link on
how to create Azure Service Principal.

Learn more   **Back**   Verify and save   ∨
Troubleshoot

Figure 7-9. *Azure DevOps new service connection for Azure Resource Manager*

Azure DevOps provides multiple different options for implementing the build and release pipelines. It provides both GUI and YAML based pipeline authoring experience. There could be separate YAML pipelines for each environment or a single multi-staged yaml pipeline targeting each environment in a stage for deployment could be authored.

Figure 7-10 shows the overall activities that are part of the build and deployment pipeline.

Figure 7-10. *Overall CI/CD process for Terraform scripts*

A multistage pipeline means that both the build and release steps are in a single YAML definition. Each stage can be configured to execute only after approval, and different steps can be performed within each stage.

A stage can have multiple jobs, and each job can have multiple tasks. Each task corresponds a particular activity within the job. The job runs on an agent instance within a given context. Another job within a stage will run on a different agent instance. Similarly, each stage and its associate jobs run on a different agent instance.

The PR and Trigger attributes help in executing the pipeline automatically in response to a change in code. The PR attribute triggers the execution of the first independent stage in the YAML pipeline for the included branches. Similarly, the Trigger attribute helps in executing the pipeline whenever code is pushed to a branch listed within its inclusion list.

The Terraform commands will be executed on an Azure DevOps agent running on Ubuntu 18.04 as part of build and release stages. There are four stages in total, as shown in Figure 7-11.

1. Building/validating Terraform scripts.

2. Deploy to the dev environment after approval.

3. Deploy to the test environment after approval.

4. Deploy to the prod environment after approval.

```
pr:
  branches:
    include: ["master", "develop"]

trigger:
- master
- develop

pool:
  vmImage: ubuntu-18.04

variables:
  folder_context: $(System.DefaultWorkingDirectory)/Terraform/environments

stages:
> - stage: terraform_build …

> - stage: development_env …

> - stage: test_env …

> - stage: prod_env …
```

Figure 7-11. *Multistage pipeline structure*

Build Stages

Figure 7-12 shows the overall build process for scripts related to Terraform.

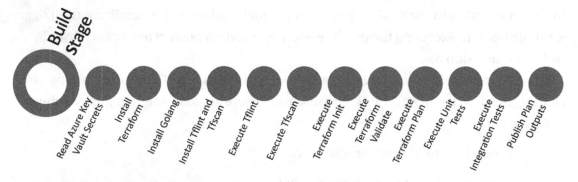

Figure 7-12. *Activities in the build stage for Terraform-related scripts*

Terraform requires service principal related information for authenticating to Azure and also the details of the storage account for storing the state file as a remote state file. These secrets are stored in the key vault and should be read as one of the first steps within the build stage.

The `AzureKeyVault` task retrieves the secrets from the key vault. It needs the name of the service connection to authenticate itself to the key vault. You will also recall that the same service principal was allowed access to secrets using the key vault access policy. The task also should know the name of the key vault to read secrets from and the names of the secret that should be read from it. The code snippet shown next, for example, retrieves the `state-resource-group` secret from the key vault. The `state-resource-group` should already exist within the key vault. This task will then access the value stored in secret using a variable with the same name as the one provided in the `secretfilter` attribute. For example, the secret `state-resource-group` can be accessed within other tasks in the same job as `$(state-resource-group)`.

```
- stage: terraform_build
  jobs:
  - job: terraform_plan
    steps:
    - task: AzureKeyVault@1
      inputs:
        azureSubscription: 'book-azure-access'
        KeyVaultName: 'book-keyvault'
        SecretsFilter: 'state-resource-group, state-storage-container,
                        state-storage-account, state-file-name, state-sas-
                        token, client-id, client-secret, subscription-id,
                        tenant-id'
      displayName: 'Get key vault secrets as pipeline variables'
```

Once we have retrieved the key vault secrets, we need to execute Terraform commands and Golang-based unit and integration tests. We also need other tools to validate and scan our Terraform scripts. The next code snippet installs Terraform version 0.14.10. It is a good practice to use version numbers in pipelines. If you download the latest version, future scripts might not be compatible with it. Having a fixed version will ensure that the script and pipeline will continue to work together even though a newer version of Terraform is available.

Notice that the `required_version` value in the Terraform HCL script is `~> 0.14`. Versioning has been explained in detail in previous chapters.

```
terraform {
  required_providers {
    azurerm = {
      source  = "hashicorp/azurerm"
      version = "=2.53.0"
    }
  }

  required_version = "~> 0.14"

    backend "azurerm" {
    resource_group_name    = "Xxx"
    storage_account_name   = "xxx"
    container_name         = "xxx"
    key                    = "xxx"
    sas_token              = "xxx"
    }
}
```

```
- bash: |
    curl -fsSL https://apt.releases.hashicorp.com/gpg | sudo apt-key add -
    sudo apt-add-repository "deb [arch=amd64] https://apt.releases.
    hashicorp.com $(lsb_release -cs) main"
    sudo apt-get update && sudo apt-get install terraform=0.14.10
    terraform -help
  displayName: 'Install Terraform'
```

The next step is to install the Golang on the agent server along with its out-of-box libraries. This is needed for unit and integration tests using the TerraTest framework. We do not need to explicitly download TerraTest framework because it gets downloaded while executing the tests. The .mod file contains all dependencies and TerraTest is one of them. It is a good practice to mention a specific version for any dependencies.

```
- task: GoTool@0
  inputs:
```

```
  version: '1.15'
displayName: 'Installing golang needed for TerraTest '
```

After the Terraform and Golang installation, the next steps are to install `tflint` and `tfsec` tools. `tflint` helps in checking the script with regard to the ruleset. The `tflint` linter is a generic linter and contains rules specific to Terraform, but it does not contain rulesets related to any plugins. Plugin rulesets should be installed after the installation of the `tflint` framework. The `tflint_ruleset_azurerm` ruleset should be installed and is shown in the next code snippet. These plugins must to installed in a folder called `.tflint.d/plugins` in the project or globally at `~/.tflint.d/plugins`. Installing them globally makes them available to all Terraform scripts. In the code snippet, it is installed globally within the system.

```
- bash: |
    curl -sL https://raw.githubusercontent.com/terraform-linters/tflint/
    master/install_linux.sh | bash

    mkdir -p ~/azurerm_linter/

    curl -Ls https://github.com/terraform-linters/tflint-ruleset-azurerm/
    releases/download/v0.12.0/tflint-ruleset-azurerm_linux_amd64.zip -o
    tflint-ruleset-azurerm_linux amd64.zip && unzip tflint-ruleset-azurerm_
    linux_amd64.zip -d ~/azurerm_linter/ && rm tflint-ruleset-azurerm_
    linux_amd64.zip

    mkdir -p ~/.tflint.d/plugins

    mv ~/azurerm_linter/tflint-ruleset-azurerm ~/.tflint.d/plugins

    curl -Ls    https://github.com/tfsec/tfsec/releases/download/v0.39.14/
    tfsec-linux-amd64 -o tfsec-linux-amd64

    chmod +x ./tfsec-linux-amd64

    sudo mv ./tfsec-linux-amd64 /usr/local/bin/tfsec
  displayName: 'Install tools for validations - tflint and tfsec along with
  tflint-ruleset-azurerm ruleset'
```

The `tfsec` framework helps in scanning the source code and validates it against security-related ruleset. If there is any violation of a rule, the task fails. The tool is moved after download to the `/usr/local/bin/tfsec` folder so that it can be executed without providing the fully qualified path.

```
- bash: |
    curl -Ls https://github.com/tfsec/tfsec/releases/download/v0.39.14/
    tfsec-linux-amd64 -o tfsec-linux-amd64
    chmod +x ./tfsec-linux-amd64
    sudo mv ./tfsec-linux-amd64 /usr/local/bin/tfsec
  displayName: 'Install tfsec'
```

After download and installing tflint, it can be executed to check for compliance, as shown in the next code snippet:

```
- bash: |
    cd $(folder_context)
    tflint ./main.tf --var-file=./varvalues/dev.tfvars --loglevel=trace
  displayName: 'Terraform tflint execution'
```

The rulesets that are applicable for the project should be enabled in a file with extension .tflint.hcl. This file should be available within the root folder of the project. This file contains the enabled rulesets for the project, and its configuration has been shown next. Few rules have been enabled for the purpose of readability; however, more rules should be enabled for a production scenario. This file is also part of the overall code files available for this chapter. The complete AzureRM-related rulesets are available at https://github.com/terraform-linters/tflint-ruleset-azurerm/tree/master/rules/apispec.

```
plugin "azurerm" {
    enabled = true
}

rule "terraform_required_version" {
  enabled = true
}

rule "terraform_comment_syntax" {
  enabled = true
}

rule "terraform_deprecated_index" {
  enabled = true
}
```

```
rule "terraform_deprecated_interpolation" {
  enabled = true
}

rule "terraform_documented_outputs" {
  enabled = true
}

rule "terraform_documented_variables" {
  enabled = true
}

rule "terraform_typed_variables" {
  enabled = true
}
```

Next, the tfsec tool is executed to check for security scan-related compliance. It does a static analysis of the Terraform scripts and fails the task if any configured rulesets are violated. The rulesets for tfsec related to Azure are available at https://tfsec.dev/docs/azure/home/.

```
- bash: |
    cd $(folder_context)
    tfsec . --tfvars-file=./varvalues/dev.tfvars --verbose
  displayName: 'Terraform security scan execution'
```

The tfsec tool can identify potential security issues in code. For example, a storage account as shown next will fail when the tfsec rulesets are run against it. The tool will complain that the minimum TLS version is not set.

```
resource "azurerm_storage_account" storage_account {
  name                     = var.storage_account_name
  resource_group_name      = module.app_resource_group.resource_group_name
  location                 = module.app_resource_group.resource_group_location
  account_tier             = "Standard"
  account_replication_type = "GRS"

  tags = {
    environment = "staging"
  }
}
```

Once the minimum TLS version for storage account is set, the validation will succeed again.

```
resource "azurerm_storage_account" storage_account {
  name                      = var.storage_account_name
  resource_group_name       = module.app_resource_group.resource_group_name
  location                  = module.app_resource_group.resource_group_location
  account_tier              = "Standard"
  account_replication_type  = "GRS"
  min_tls_version = "TLS1_2"

  tags = {
    environment = "staging"
  }
}
```

The next code snippet executes Terraform commands, specifically, the `init` and `plan` commands for each environment. Since we have three environments, the Terraform code checkout is copied three times, one for each environment, and `init` and `plan` are executed for each of the environment in their respective folders. This ensures a separate state file is generated for each environment in a remote state stored in a storage blob container. The commands also utilize the secrets from the key vault by passing them as variables to the Terraform script. Each `plan` command generates a separate plan file for each environment in the `outputs` folder, which will eventually be published as a build artifact. This plan file will be utilized in subsequent deployment stages within the pipeline.

```
- bash: |

    cp -rf $(System.DefaultWorkingDirectory)/Terraform/ $(System.
    DefaultWorkingDirectory)/dev
    cp -rf $(System.DefaultWorkingDirectory)/Terraform/ $(System.
    DefaultWorkingDirectory)/test
    cp -rf $(System.DefaultWorkingDirectory)/Terraform/ $(System.
    DefaultWorkingDirectory)/prod

    mkdir -p $(System.DefaultWorkingDirectory)/Terraform/outputs

    cd $(System.DefaultWorkingDirectory)/dev/environments
    echo $(pwd)
    echo $(ls)
```

```
terraform init -backend-config='resource_group_name=$(state-resource-
group)' -backend-config='storage_account_name=$(state-storage-account)'
-backend-config='container_name=$(state-storage-container)' -backend-
config='key=ci-dev.tfstate' -backend-config='sas_token=$(state-sas-
token)' -force-copy

terraform plan -var-file=./varvalues/dev.tfvars -var='client_
id=$(client-id)' -var='client_secret=$(client-secret)' -var='tenant_
id=$(tenant-id)' -var='subscription_id=$(subscription-id)'
-out='$(System.DefaultWorkingDirectory)/Terraform/outputs/
dev.plan' -input=false

cd $(System.DefaultWorkingDirectory)/test/environments
terraform init -backend-config='resource_group_name=$(state-resource-
group)' -backend-config='storage_account_name=$(state-storage-account)'
-backend-config='container_name=$(state-storage-container)' -backend-
config='key=ci-test.tfstate' -backend-config='sas_token=$(state-sas-
token)' -force-copy

terraform plan -var-file=./varvalues/test.tfvars -var='client_
id=$(client-id)' -var='client_secret=$(client-secret)' -var='tenant_
id=$(tenant-id)' -var='subscription_id=$(subscription-id)'
-out='$(System.DefaultWorkingDirectory)/Terraform/outputs/test.plan'
-input=false

cd $(System.DefaultWorkingDirectory)/prod/environments
terraform init -backend-config='resource_group_name=$(state-resource-
group)' -backend-config='storage_account_name=$(state-storage-account)'
-backend-config='container_name=$(state-storage-container)' -backend-
config='key=ci-prod.tfstate' -backend-config='sas_token=$(state-sas-
token)' -force-copy

terraform plan -var-file=./varvalues/prod.tfvars -var='client_
id=$(client-id)' -var='client_secret=$(client-secret)' -var='tenant_
id=$(tenant-id)' -var='subscription_id=$(subscription-id)'
-out='$(System.DefaultWorkingDirectory)/Terraform/outputs/prod.plan'
-input=false
displayName: 'Executing Terraform commands'
```

As part of validating the correctness of Terraform modules, unit tests should be executed against them so that any issues with them can be identified and detected up front. If any test case fails, the entire unit test task fails. The next chapter covers testing Terraform scripts in depth with the process of Unit and Integration testing Terraform scripts. Terraform scripts can be tested using the TerraTest framework written in Golang. The unit tests for the purpose of this chapter are also written in Golang.

```bash
- bash: |
    cd $(System.DefaultWorkingDirectory)/Terraform/tests/unittests
    go test ./...  -v -subscription_id $(subscription-id) -client_id
    $(client-id) -tenant_id $(tenant-id) -client_secret $(client-secret)
  displayName: 'Executing TerraTest unit test scripts'
```

As part of validating the correctness of Terraform scripts that brings multiple resources together, Integration tests should be executed so that any issues with the code can be identified and detected up front just like with unit tests. The differences between integration and unit tests are the scope and the purpose of test. The integration tests bring multiple resources together and validate if they work together as intended. If any test case fails, the entire Integration task fails. This aspect of Terraform is also covered in next chapter.

```bash
- bash: |
    cd $(System.DefaultWorkingDirectory)/Terraform/tests/integrationtests
    go test ./...  -v -subscription_id $(subscription-id) -client_id
    $(client-id) -tenant_id $(tenant-id) -client_secret $(client-secret)
    -state_resource_group $(state-resource-group)  -state_storage_account
    $(state-storage-account)  -state_storage_container $(state-storage-
    container) -state_file_name $(state-file-name) -state_sas_token
    $(state-sas-token)
  displayName: 'Executing TerraTest integration test scripts'
```

The last step in the build stage is to publish the folder consisting of Terraform plan outputs for each environment. It is done using the PublishBuildArtifact task. It needs a name and an output path to which the artifacts will be published.

```
- task: PublishBuildArtifacts@1
  inputs:
    pathToPublish: '$(System.DefaultWorkingDirectory)/Terraform/outputs'
    artifactName: environments
```

Release/Deployment Stages

After the build stage is complete, the Terraform scripts are valid and in compliance with the standards set within the project. Note that the entire build stage was involved in the validation and verification of the Terraform scripts. It actually never executes the Terraform scripts to provision any environment. The next stage after build stage is to execute the Terraform scripts to provision the development environment. We already have generated the Terraform plan file in the build stage for each environment, so essentially we just need to initialize the Terraform environment and apply the generated Terraform plan. We already know that the initialization of Terraform environment involves downloading and installing plugins and modules used within the scripts. This mandates that either the entire Terraform script source code is available to this stage or the modules can be downloaded from well-defined URI's like GitHub.

Since the stage is related to deployment targeted to the development environment, the dev environment provisioned earlier as part of preparation steps would be the target of the deployment. The dev environment is configured with manual approval, so the pipeline will halt after the build stage is complete and wait for approval. Only after getting the approval, the development_env stage will start to execute.

Figure 7-13 shows the activities to be executed as part of the deployment stage.

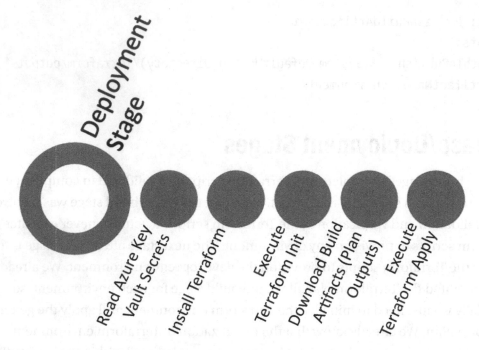

Figure 7-13. *Deployment stages for Terraform scripts*

```
- stage: development_env
  jobs:
  - deployment: development_environment
    displayName: development_environment
    pool:
      vmImage: Ubuntu-18.04
    environment: dev
    strategy:
      runOnce:
        deploy:
          steps:
          - checkout: self

          - task: AzureKeyVault@1
            inputs:
              azureSubscription: 'book-azure-access'
              KeyVaultName: 'book-keyvault'
```

```
      SecretsFilter: 'state-resource-group, state-storage-
        container, state-storage-account, state-file-name, state-sas-
        token, client-id, client-secret, subscription-id, tenant-id'
      displayName: 'Get key vault secrets as pipeline variables'

  - bash: |
      curl -fsSL https://apt.releases.hashicorp.com/gpg | sudo
      apt-key add -
      sudo apt-add-repository "deb [arch=amd64] https://apt.
      releases.hashicorp.com $(lsb_release -cs) main"
      sudo apt-get update && sudo apt-get install terraform=0.14.10
      terraform -help
    displayName: 'Install Terraform'

  - task: DownloadBuildArtifacts@0
    inputs:
      buildType: 'current'
      downloadType: 'single'
      artifactName: 'environments'
      downloadPath: '$(Build.SourcesDirectory)/Terraform'

  - bash: |
      cd '$(Build.SourcesDirectory)/Terraform/environments'
      terraform init -backend-config='resource_group_name=
      $(state-resource-group)' -backend-config='storage_account_
      name=$(state-storage-account)' -backend-config='container_
      name=$(state-storage-container)' -backend-config='key=dev.
      tfstate' -backend-config='sas_token=$(state-sas-token)'
      terraform apply './dev.plan'
    displayName: 'Executing Terraform apply commands'
```

The first task in the dev stage is to Git clone the source files from repository using the checkout task. This will ensure that the source code is available in this stage to the agent and the Terraform init command can be executed against them. However, the Terraform init command is dependent on secrets stored in Azure Key Vault, and they should be retrieved prior to the execution of Terraform commands. Secrets related to the service principal and access to remote storage account for state management are retrieved from key vault.

We require the Terraform executable for executing the Terraform commands and so Terraform version 0.14.10 is installed. The only artifact missing now before the Terraform `apply` command can be executed is the plan output file for this environment. Remember that this file is available as part of the published artifacts from the build stage. In the development environment stage, using the `DownloadBuildArtifacts` task, the plan output file can be obtained and accessed.

An important consideration to note while using Terraform commands such as `init` and `apply` is that they are executed from the `environments` folder. This folder contains the main Terraform scripts that are responsible for provisioning the environment. This folder also contains the plugins and module declaration needed by the `terraform init` command. We also wanted to download the plan output file (the ones generated and published from build stage) in this directory, although this is not a hard requirement. This was to avoid unnecessary switching of folder context, to extract plan files in the same folder as rest of the Terraform scripts. For this to happen, both the publish artifact and download artifact tasks are named `"environments"` because the name of the download artifact task will become part of the file path and so it will download and extract all files within the `environments` folder.

Finally, the `terraform apply` command with the `dev.plan` file is executed from within the `environments` folder.

Similar to the `development_env` stage, multiple stages—one for each environment—can be part of the YAML pipeline to provision environments like the test and production.

Whenever a stage related to deployment is going to get initiated, it will halt to manual approval requirement. This is shown in Figure 7-14. Here, the `test_env` stage is waiting for approval after completion of `development_env`. Once the approver clicks the Review button and approves the execution, the `test_env` stage will continue execution.

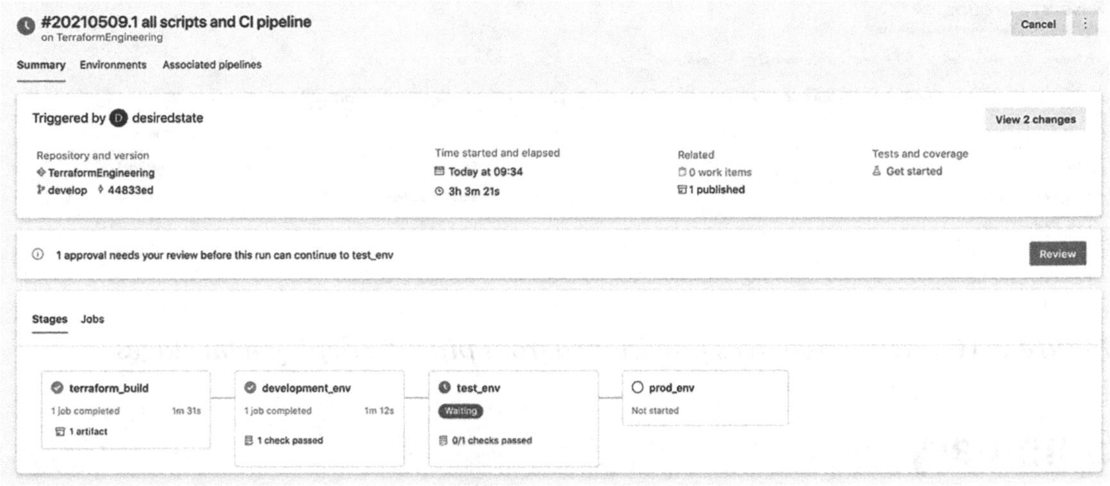

Figure 7-14. *Manual approval between deployment stages*

Eventually once all the stages are executed, the pipeline will look like the one shown in Figure 7-15.

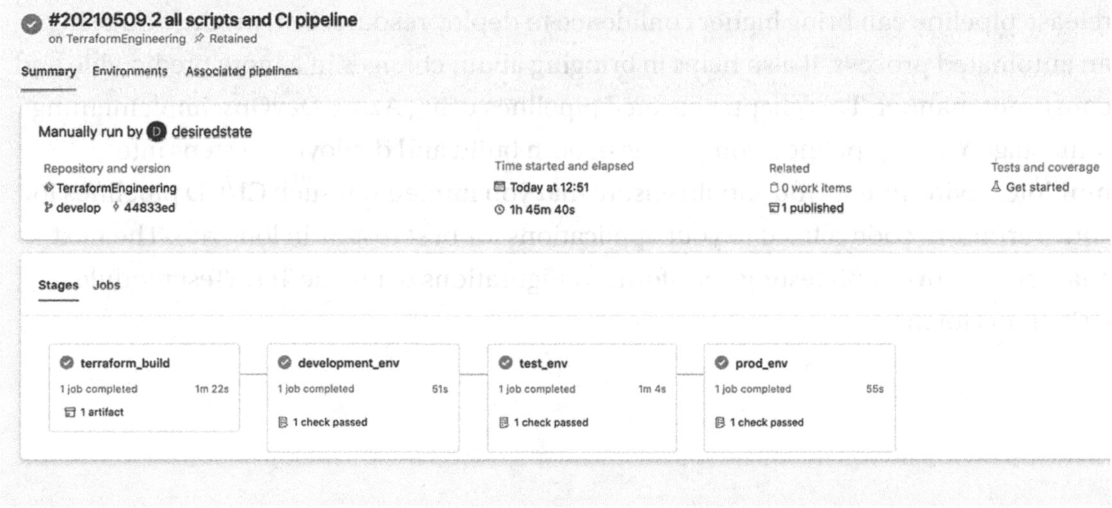

Figure 7-15. *Pipeline execution run status*

The final resource output can be viewed from the Azure portal, as shown in Figure 7-16. Notice that three resource groups, one corresponding to each deployment stage, are provisioned. The values for these resource configurations have been derived from the Terraform tfvars file available as part of the source code.

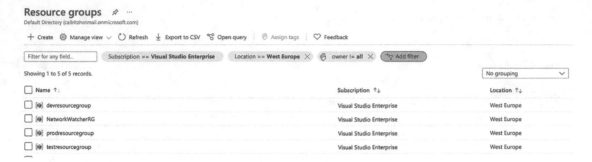

Figure 7-16. *Azure resources provisioned from pipeline deployment stages*

Summary

In this chapter, CI/CD pipelines were introduced that had tasks and steps specific to Terraform-based build and deployment of environments. Terraform provides quite a versatile and mature ecosystem of tools and frameworks for enabling automated build including steps to check and validate Terraform scripts, unit and integration testing, using `tflint`, static security scanning using `tfsec`. A well-defined build and release pipeline can bring higher confidence to deploy resources on production using an automated process. It also helps in bringing about changes in a more predictable and consistent manner. This chapter covered pipelines using Azure DevOps, implementing multistage YAML pipelines, comprising of both build and deployment steps into multiple environment. You should ensure that you implement such CI/CD pipelines for your Terraform code related to your applications for best results in long run. The next chapter will cover unit testing Terraform configurations using the TerraTest module written in Golang.

CHAPTER 8

Terraform Unit Testing

Terraform is quite unique and different when it comes to testing. In normal situations with other programming languages, it is easy to test the code in isolation and also together—thanks to the abundant availability of libraries and frameworks that help in creating context for different kinds of tests and that help determine the quality of code and application.

Terraform, as you well know by now, is based on the principles of Infrastructure as Code (IaC). Terraform code actually performs an external action like invoking an Azure API to do its job. The job of Terraform is to generate and manage resources in a remote cloud environment.

Introduction to Unit Testing

Software engineering is not a new practice, and almost all enterprises have some degree of maturity to take their applications and services on a journey to production. One part of this journey is testing, and there are many different types of tests. These tests focus on validating the quality of deliverables from different points of view. While most tests are focused on the functionality, performance, and security of the application, a couple of tests are focused on the application code. These are the unit and integration tests.

Unit tests means testing one unit of the code, and it is therefore important to define a *unit* from a code perspective. Remember that unit testing is related to code. A unit could be a line of code, a block of code, a function, or a class, and we can keep going into higher abstractions. As a practice, a function is generally regarded as a unit, and so each function should undergo unit testing to validate them.

However, what does unit testing mean? *Unit testing* is the process of validating that the code is working as expected. This means we should know what the expectation from the target function is before we write the unit test in different situations.

© Ritesh Modi 2021
R. Modi, *Deep-Dive Terraform on Azure*, https://doi.org/10.1007/978-1-4842-7328-9_8

Once we know the expected outcomes in different scenarios, we can compare each of them with the actual outcome in the unit test. If both the outcomes match, the test succeeds; otherwise, it fails.

Another important aspect of unit testing is that the test is solely focused on the target function. If the target function is dependent on other functions, those other functions should not be part of the current tests testing the function. There should be other tests that conduct testing on those helper or child functions. This can impose a challenge because the target function is already invoking other functions. In such cases, mocking and faking concepts are used to mock the dependencies rather than actual invocation, and there are multiple frameworks that help in implementing them.

The process of unit testing starts with documenting the requirements, writing unit test cases, and then either following test-driven development or interactively implementing test cases along with the application. It is a good practice to adopt test-driven development and implement unit tests iteratively while coding the application.

Generally, multiple unit tests are written against a function covering all its code paths, ensuring that positive and negative cases and exceptions have been accounted for.

There is a well-defined pattern known as Assemble-Act-Assertion available for writing the unit tests. This pattern has three distinct phases (Assemble, Act and Assert) for any implementation of unit tests.

In simple words, code at the beginning of the unit test should "assemble" the artifacts that are eventually needed and consumed from both Act and Assertion phase. Assemble typically consists of generating the expected values for later comparison with the actual values. It generates any input parameters for the target function and other activities deemed necessary for executing the target function.

Act is the next part of code within a unit test, and it is responsible for invoking the target function, passing in input values, and capturing outputs and errors.

Assertion is where the decision whether the unit test passes or fails is made. In this part of code, comparisons between the expected and actual outcomes are made, and based on the result, the test either succeeds or fails.

Application vs. Infrastructure Unit Testing

Unit testing is quite prominent for applications and is gaining momentum for the infrastructure domain. Infrastructure traditionally was a manual activity with some support from scripting and hence never got any attention with regard to testing in general. However, with the origin of the IaC paradigm and availability of tools and frameworks to implement IaC, many enterprises are already conducting unit tests before infrastructure deployments.

This book is about Terraform, so the focus will be on testing IaC. Terratest is one of the leading open source tools for authoring and executing both unit and integration tests for Terraform.

Introduction to Terratest

Terratest (https://terratest.gruntwork.io/) is an open source Golang-based library meant for testing IaC. Terratest helps automate tests against code written using Terraform. Terratest is quite a versatile library consisting of multiple modules, each responsible for providing a rich infrastructure for writing comprehensive unit, integration, and end-to-end tests.

Since Terratest is dependent on Go, it should be installed prior to using it. Go can be downloaded from the https://golang.org/dl/ website, and Terratest requires a 1.13 minimum version.

Once Go is installed, Terratest can be installed using the go get command, as shown here:

```
go get github.com/gruntwork-io/terratest
```

Once Terratest is installed on the local machine, it can be used for writing and executing tests against Terraform scripts.

Writing the First Unit Test Using Terratest

Visual Studio Code is a great tool and editor for writing Terraform-related test cases. Generally, Terraform scripts are stored in a folder different from the testing scripts. We will create a new folder on the filesystem and open the code editor in the context of this newly created folder. Within this folder, create another set of two folders: fixtures and tests.

The folder `fixtures` will consist of Terraform scripts, and `tests` will contain Golang code for tests written using the Terratest library. The tests will consume the scripts in the `fixture` folder.

Within the `fixture` folder, copy the Terraform script with the code listing shown next. This code is quite simple- it `provisions` a resource group on Azure, and it uses client credentials authentication. It accepts six variables (in other languages these are known as *parameters*); they are the resource group name and its location, `client_id, subscription_id,` `tenant_id,` and `client_secret`. It has two outputs: one returns resource group name and the other it's unique ID.

```
variable rg_name { type = string }
variable location {type= string }
variable client_id {type= string }
variable subscription_id {type= string }
variable tenant_id {type= string }
variable client_secret {type= string }

provider "azurerm" {
    client_id = var.client_id
    client_secret = var.client_secret
    subscription_id = var.subscription_id
    tenant_id = var.tenant_id
    features {}
}

resource "azurerm_resource_group" "rgdemo" {
  name     = var.rg_name
  location = var.location
}

output rg_identifier {
    value = azurerm_resource_group.rgdemo.name
}

output rg_id {
    value = azurerm_resource_group.rgdemo.id
}
```

Next, we will focus on writing our first unit test. The unit test will be responsible for executing the Terraform configuration.

We will navigate to the Terminal section of Visual Studio Code and ensure that we are in the context of the `tests` folder. The test code is written in Golang, so it is a good practice to initialize a module by executing the following command:

```
go mod init firsttest
```

This command will create (initiate) a new module named `firsttest`. It will generate a new `go.mod` file, which is the module manifest file providing metadata information about the module.

Now, we can start writing our first test. We will create a new Go file named `first_test.go`. Notice that the name of the file ends with `_test`. This nomenclature is used by the Go `test` command to pick up test files automatically at runtime while executing tests.

The first line of code defines a new package followed by the import libraries needed for test purposes:

```
package basictests

import (
    "os"
    "testing"
    "fmt"
    "github.com/gruntwork-io/terratest/modules/random"
    "github.com/gruntwork-io/terratest/modules/terraform"
    "github.com/stretchr/testify/assert"
)
```

The Golang testing package has the core test related features helping in writing and executing automated tests using the Go language. It "Go Test" provides the functionality to execute Go tests within files that have `_test` as the suffix in their names. It also executes any function with a name that starts with Test within test files. In short, creating `*_test.go` files containing functions starting with Test* are executed using the Go `test` command.

"Terraform" is one of the core Terratest packages that provides the basic plumbing to test infrastructure code in terms of configuring the test, generating the Terraform command, executing, and fetching outputs. These are core operation in any tests with regard to Terraform.

"Assert" is another important library that provides functions for comparing the actual and expected values and this activity eventually decides whether the test fails or passes. It has multiple comparison functions for different scenarios, and we will cover some of the major ones in this chapter.

A random package is used to generate random values and is an important package for testing Terraform scripts. It helps in passing dynamic values to variables in Terraform scripts, making the test generic and ensuring that the tests do not fail due to hard-coded of names and identifiers. The names and identifiers are generally unique within a cloud environment, and using random names and identifiers for each test run eliminates the possibility of name conflicts with other runs by the same developer or any other developer.

"os" and "fmt" are standard Golang-provided packages. os helps in working with the operating system, and fmt helps in formatting the text as well for providing stdin and stdout functionality.

However, the packages mentioned earlier might not already be available within the local system. One way to install these packages is to execute the command that will download these packages in a local folder named vendor. The command should be executed from within the tests folder, and that command is shown next.

```
Go mod vendor
```

The function signature shown next implements the unit tests for our target Terraform script. Notice that it starts with Test as part of its name. The function accepts a pointer to struct T defined within the testing package. The Terratest runtime is responsible for creating an instance of this struct and passing it to the function when the tests execute. Every test should accept T struct as a parameter without which the tests will not execute. This structure is used internally by the Go test to manage the state of running tests and also helps in generating and formatting log data.

```
func TestResourceGroup(t *testing.T) {

}
```

By now we understand the Arrange-Act-Assert pattern for unit testing; the next code listing is implemented as part of the function that helps in the Arrange part of the test.

The first few lines of code declare variables containing values and used later in the function as expected values for the test. There are two unit tests within this function (although there can be many more). This is just an illustration about how to write and execute unit tests against Terraform scripts.

- Testing the resource group name

- Testing the resource group identifier

The first line of code generates a six-character random text. This will be used as the name of the resource group for the test and will be supplied as a value to the rg_name variable.

The resource group identifier is a string value that is unique within Azure and is in URI format. It formed as a combination of subscription id and resource group name. Since subscriptionId is sensitive data, it should not be hard-coded within the test code; rather, the test should either get this value as input variable or environmental variable. Similarly, other sensitive data like Client_ID, Client_Secret, and Tenant_Id should be supplied to the tests. It must be ensured that the environmental variables SUBSCRIPTION_ID, TENANT_ID, CLIENT_ID, and CLIENT_SECRET exist before executing the test. These values are needed such that Terraform can authenticate itself to Azure. They could be hard-coded within the test code; however, this is sensitive information and should not be part of code files that can be read by anyone having access to them. These values should be supplied to the Terraform configuration for each declared variable. Using the value stored within the SUBSCRIPTION_ID environment variable and the resourceGroupName variable, the expected resource group identifier string is generated using the Sprintf function from the fmt package.

After the Arrange part of the unit test that generates and arranges expected values and parameters to be supplied to the Terraform script, the next step is to configure the Terraform options with appropriate configuration values.

Remember that Terratest is a wrapper over the Terraform CLI. It generates the CLI commands based on the configuration options supplied to it. The Terraform configuration is implemented as a struct named "options" within the terraform package. There are quite a few configuration options; however, for this example, we will just use couple of them. The TerraformDir attribute refers to the location of the Terraform script that is under test, and it is a mandatory configuration. The vars attribute helps in suppling parameter values to variables declared within the Terraform script.

```
// Setting resource group configuration, including name and rg_
    identifier
// the subscriptionId, clientId, Client_secret and tenantId is not
    hard-coded in script. Rather it is read as environmental variable
resourceGroupName := random.UniqueId()
```

```
subscriptionID := os.Getenv("SUBSCRIPTION_ID")
clientID := os.Getenv("Client_ID")
tenantID := os.Getenv("Tenant_ID")
clientSecret := os.Getenv("Client_Secret")
resourceGroupId := fmt.Sprintf("/subscriptions/%s/resourceGroups/%s",
subscriptionID,resourceGroupName)

// Terraform configuration used for the test. This helps in generating
   the Terraform command
terraformOptions := &terraform.Options{
    // The path to where our Terraform code is located
    TerraformDir: "../fixtures",

    // Variables to pass to our Terraform code using -var options
    Vars: map[string]interface{}{
        "rg_name":  resourceGroupName,
        "location": "west europe",
        "client_id" : clientID,
        "client_secret" : clientSecret,
        "subscription_id" : subscriptionID,
        "tenant_id" : tenantID,
    },
}
```

After the Assemble stage, the focus moves to the Act stage of the test. Act means to take an action, and in our context, it refers to the execution of a Terraform script to provision resources in the cloud environment. The Terratest Terraform package provides multiple functions related to initialization, planning, and applying of the Terraform configuration. In the code listing shown next, the Terraform InitAndPlan method initializes the Terraform environment (it downloads the azurerm plugin and any dependent modules) and also executes the "plan" command for the target script. After the plan execution, the apply function is invoked, which helps in provisioning the resources defined in Terraform script. You will notice that almost all the functions within Terratest accept testing pointer as parameter. The struct instance is its first parameter, and the "option" struct is the second parameter.

The first line of code is quite interesting, and it uses a Golang feature to defer the execution of code to the end of the function. "defer" in Golang ensures that the corresponding line of code or function is executed as the last line of code, although it is not mentioned as the last line. It can be defined anywhere within the function. Generally, all cleanup activities are executed as part of the defer code. Since it is a good practice to leave the environment before and after testing in the same state, it is prudent to tear down all the resources provisioned as part of the test execution. This will ensure that the cloud costs do not keep increasing with more test execution, and the cloud environment also remains clean of unwanted resources. Terraform "destroy" function helps in removing the provisioned resource as the last step within the test.

```
// This will cleanup all resources provisioned as part of test as final step
defer terraform.Destroy(t, terraformOptions)
```

```
// This will init and plan the resources and fail the test if there are
   any errors
terraform.InitAndPlan(t, terraformOptions)
```

```
// This will apply the resources and fail the test if there are any errors
terraform.Apply(t, terraformOptions)
```

Next comes the crux of any unit testing where the expected values are compared with actual values, and this stage is known as the Assert stage. In this stage, the actual values are extracted (the actual values should be available by now as the previous stage has already executed the scripts and the scripts have generated the output values) as output from the Terraform script. We also already have the expected values as part of the Arrange stage. To extract output from the Terraform execution, the Terraform package provides multiple output functions. The most used one is the Output function, which again accepts the T struct and Terraform configuration options along with the name of the output we are interested in and have declared within the Terraform script. It will contain the runtime generated value as part of the Terraform script execution. The output functions are wrapped over the Terraform output CLI command. There are multiple variations available for output functions, each intended for different purposes; see Table 8-1.

Table 8-1. *Output Functions*

Output Function	Description
Output	Invokes the Terraform output command and works with Terraform primitive types. It returns string values for the string, number, and bool datatypes. Does not fail the test if the returned value is empty.
OutputRequired	Invokes the Terraform output command and works with Terraform primitive types. It returns string values for the string, number, and bool datatypes. It fails the test if the return value is empty.
OutputMap	Returns the Golang map object map[string]interface {}. The keys are type string, and the values could be any type returned by the output.
OutputList	Returns the Golang slice object []string.
OutputMapOfObjects	Returns a Golang map object containing Terraform objects with multiple name-value pairs. They are equivalent to a map of JSON objects.
OutputListOfObjects	Returns a Golang slice object containing Terraform objects with multiple name-value pairs. They are equivalent to a JSON array of objects.

In the code shown next, the name of the resource group and its identifier are extracted using the Output function. Both of these values are defined in a Terraform script as output blocks.

```
// This will pull output values generated as part of Terraform script
   execution
rg_identifier := terraform.Output(t, terraformOptions, "rg_identifier")
rg_id := terraform.Output(t, terraformOptions, "rg_id")

// Comparing the actual and expected values. Fail is they do not match
assert.Equal(t, resourceGroupName, rg_identifier)
assert.Equal(t, resourceGroupId, rg_id)
```

Once we get the actual values, the asset package has an Equal function that takes a T struct, the expected value, and the actual value. If they both match, the test passes; otherwise, it fails.

There are different types of assertions available within the Assert package. An "equal" assertion checks for equality, while the other functions are for performing other types of comparisons. Table 8-2 lists the most important assertion functions.

Table 8-2. *Assertion Functions Available in Assert Library*

Assertion Function	Description
Equal	Equal checks if the expected and actual objects are equal.
isEmpty	This function checks if the output value is empty. It returns true if it is empty.
Len	Len checks the length of the output and compares it with the specified length.
False/True	False checks if the output is Boolean False. True is just the opposite of it.
NotEqual	This is opposite of the Equal function. It returns true if the two objects are not equal.
Contains	Returns true if a string/list/map contains a specified substring/element/key.
Panics	Fails the test if the output is a panic (exception in other languages).

After authoring the first test, it can now be executed to unit test the target Terraform script. To execute the test, again ensure that you are in the tests folder and execute the command shown here:

```
SUBSCRIPTION_ID=xxxxx-xxxx-xxxx-xxxxxxxxxxxx CLIENT_ID=xxxxxxxx-
xxxx-xxxx-xxxxxxxx TENANT_ID=xxxxxxxx-xxxx-xxxx-xxxxxxxx CLIENT_
SECRET=xxxxxxxxxxxxxxxxxxx go test -v
```

This command adds subscription_id, client_id, client_secret, and tenant_id as environment variables for the scope of the current command. You should provide a valid value for these environment variables while executing this command. The Go test command finds the files that end with _test as part of filename and the functions that start with Test as part of the function name. Out TestResourceGroup function will get picked up and executed. The three stages of Arrange, Act, and Assert will be executed one after another, and finally we will get the log output that shows whether the test succeeded or failed. The -v option ensures verbose output is generated while executing the tests.

The partial output from the test is shown next:

```
TestResourceGroup 2021-07-03T20:42:11+05:30 logger.go:66: Destroy complete!
Resources: 1 destroyed.
TestResourceGroup 2021-07-03T20:42:11+05:30 logger.go:66:
--- PASS: TestResourceGroup (163.54s)
PASS
ok      firsttest       164.074s
```

Astute readers might have noticed that in our previous test function, the test passes or fails based on the outcome of the assert functions. If we want to have more control over the outcome of the test apart from the assert functions, the Golang testing framework provides functions to do so. See Table 8-3.

***Table 8-3.** Functions to Set Test Status*

Assertion Function	Description
Fail	This function will not stop execution of the function. The function execution will continue, but the eventual test result will be failure.
Log	This function logs a message to the stdout stream with the text message provided.
Error	This function will log the message and mark the test as a failure. It will not stop the execution.
Fatal	This function will log the message and mark the test as a failure. It will also stop the execution.
skip	This function will skip the test from further execution and mark the test as complete.

Testing Multiple Terraform Resources Generated Using count

In this section, we will add a new resource block to the existing Terraform script that provisions multiple resource groups using the count property. The block shown next generates two resource groups with the names RGCount-0 and RGCount-1.

```
resource "azurerm_resource_group" "CountExample" {
  count = 2
  name      = "RGCount-${count.index}"
  location = var.location
}
```

An output block that outputs the full configuration related to CountExample is shown next:

```
output all_resource_groups {
    value = azurerm_resource_group.CountExample
}
```

Now, let's add tests for unit testing the CountExample resource. We already know by now from the previous chapters that Count generates a list of resources. These resources can use an index. Please refer to Chapter 4 for more information about the Count property.

The updated assert code for the test is shown next:

```
// This will pull output values generated as part of Terraform script
    execution
rg_identifier := terraform.Output(t, terraformOptions, "rg identifier")
rg_id := terraform.Output(t, terraformOptions, "rg_id")
```

**all_resource_groups := terraform.OutputListOfObjects(t,
terraformOptions,   "all_resource_groups")**

```
// Comparing the actual and expected values. Fail is they do not match
assert.Equal(t, resourceGroupName, rg_identifier)
assert.Equal(t, resourceGroupId, rg_id)
```

assert.Equal(t, "RGCount-0", all_resource_groups[0]["name"])

The code adds an additional function calls for reading the Terraform output; however, this time the output is not a simple string but a list of resources (objects). There is a specialized function called "OutputListOfObjects" just for this purpose. It returns the configuration for all the resources as a list.

The assertion code checks the expected and actual values by indexing and retrieving an individual property. To assert on all the resources within the list, a for loop can be used to navigate through all the objects. This is shown in the next code listing. Here, a slice containing two string values, both representing the expected name for resource groups, is declared, and an assertion within a loop and over the list containing the resource group configuration will ensure that all the resources are evaluated.

```
rglist := []string{"RGCount-0", "RGCount-1"}

for i, rggroups := range all_resource_groups {
    assert.Equal(t, rglist[i], rggroups["name"])
}
```

Testing Multiple Terraform Resources Generated Using for_each

In this section, we will again add a new resource block to the existing Terraform script that provisions multiple resource groups using the for_each property. The block shown next generates two resource groups with the name maprg-0 at the west europe location and maprg -1 at the east us location. A variable of type map(string) is also added to the script with default values.

```
variable rgnames {
    type = map(string)
    default = {
        "maprg-1": "west europe",
        "maprg-2": "east us"
    }
}

resource "azurerm_resource_group" "ForeachExample" {
  for_each = var.rgnames
  name      = each.key
  location = each.value
}
```

Here is an output block that outputs the entire configuration related to ForeachExample:

```
output all_resource_groups_map {
    value = azurerm_resource_group.ForeachExample
}
```

Now, let's add tests for unit testing the CountExample resource again. We already know by now from the previous chapters that for_each generates a map with key-value pairs. The values within the map can be accessed using the key. Please refer to Chapter 4 for more information on for_each.

The updated assert code for the test is shown here:

```
// This will pull output values generated as part of Terraform script
   execution
rg_identifier := terraform.Output(t, terraformOptions, "rg_identifier")
rg_id := terraform.Output(t, terraformOptions, "rg_id")
```

```
all_resource_groups := terraform.OutputMapOfObjects(t,
terraformOptions,    "all_resource_groups")
```

```
// Comparing the actual and expected values. Fail is they do not match
assert.Equal(t, resourceGroupName, rg_identifier)
assert.Equal(t, resourceGroupId, rg_id)
```

```
rgmapvalues := map[string]string{
    "maprg-1": "westeurope",
    "maprg-2": "eastus",
}
```

```
for key, val := range MapofResourceGroups {

    temp, _ := val.(map[string]interface{})
    assert.Equal(t, temp["location"], rgmapvalues[key])

}
```

The code adds an additional function invocation for reading the Terraform output; however, this time the output is not a simple string but a map of resources or in other words a map of objects. There is another specialized function called "OutputMapOfObjects" just for this purpose. It returns the resource configuration as a Golang map.

To assert on all the resources within the map, a for loop is used to navigate through all the objects in the map. A specific property location from within the map of objects is compared with the expected values declared within a local variable called rgmapvalues.

Working with Remote State

Terraform is heavily dependent on state files to identify changes in remote cloud environments after identifying differences after comparing the local Terraform script. By default, the state files are generated and stored on the local filesystem; however, almost all Terraform scripts make use of remote backend to store the state file remotely such that it can be shared with multiple developers and managed centrally. The remote backend configuration is part of the Terraform script and is placed within the Terraform block, as shown next:

```
terraform {
  backend "azurerm" {
    resource_group_name    = "Xxxx"
    storage_account_name   = "Xxxx"
    container_name         = "Xxxx"
    key                    = "Xxxx"
    access_key             = "Xxxx"
  }
}
```

As we know by now, the Terraform block is one of the first blocks to get executed during execution, even before the variables and locals are evaluated. This means we cannot use variables to make them generic by supplying values at runtime. Hard-coding these values in a script is not a good practice either. The values for Terraform backend properties are supplied using a `backend-config` option available with the Terraform `init` command.

One of the solutions, which is also a good practice, is to use environment variables to provide values for sensitive information like access keys or SAS tokens to the backend configuration.

Both of these approaches should be used together with Terratest to ensure that Terraform is appropriately configured before executing the `plan` and `apply` commands from the test script.

1. Using environment variables

2. Using the `backend-config` option with the `init` command

The next code listing shows how to use both environment variable and BackendConfig to supply values to the Terraform azurerm back end at runtime.

The first few lines read the environment variables related to the storage account name, container name, storage account resource group name, and name for state file, and they are stored in local variables. These environment variables should exist before running the test containing the code listed here:

```
// reading environment variables needed for remote state.
    // These must be set prior to execution of the test
    state_rgname := os.Getenv("STATE_RGNAME")
    state_storagename := os.Getenv("STATE_STORAGENAME")
    state_containername := os.Getenv("STATE_CONTAINERNAME")
    state_filename := os.Getenv("STATE_FILENAME")
    resourceGroupName := random.UniqueId()
    subscriptionID := os.Getenv("SUBSCRIPTION_ID")
    clientID := os.Getenv("Client_ID")
    tenantID := os.Getenv("Tenant_ID")
    clientSecret := os.Getenv("Client_Secret")
    resourceGroupId := fmt.Sprintf("/subscriptions/%s/resourceGroups/%s",
    subscriptionID,resourceGroupName)

    terraformOptions := &terraform.Options{
        // The path to where our Terraform code is located
        TerraformDir: "../fixtures",

        // Variables to pass to our Terraform code using -var options
        Vars: map[string]interface{}{
            "rg_name":  resourceGroupName,
            "location": "west europe",
            "client_id" : clientID,
            "client_secret" : clientSecret,
            "subscription_id" : subscriptionID,
            "tenant_id" : tenantID,
        },

        // variables meant for init command only
        BackendConfig: map[string]interface{}{
            "resource_group_name":  state_rgname,
```

```
        "storage_account_name": state_storagename,
        "container_name":       state_containername,
        "key":                  state_filename,
    },

    EnvVars: map[string]string{
        "ARM_ACCESS_KEY": "Xxxxxx
    },
}
```

Next is the code for configuring the Options struct. It contains the familiar Terraform Dir and Vars properties, and it also has a couple of new properties. The BackendConfig is used to provide values to the init command. It provides the storage account resource group name, storage account name, container name, and state filename. It does not provide any value for access keys or SAS tokens, which are needed to secure access to Azure blob storage. The access token is supplied using the EnvVars property, which creates new environment variables and assigns values to them. Even access and account keys should be supplied using environment variables. This example used the access key along with EnvVars property to show its usage. In fact, just creating an "ARM_ACCESS_KEY" environment variable within current context will ensure Terraform picks it automatically and it need not be passed to it explicitly.

Both BackendConfig and EnvVars are of the map[string]string type, which means they can accept any number of key-value pairs of type string each.

Multiple Subtests Within a Test

Now that we understand how to write unit tests for Terraform scripts, executing them from the command line, one of the important considerations is how the tests should be organized.

Should we put all assert statements within a single test? Should there be separate test functions for each assert statement? Can multiple tests be executed in parallel?

The previous example implemented multiple assert statements within a single Test function. In effect, it generated and executed a single test, and that was evident from the output from the test execution. To recap the execution output, it is being shown again here:

```
TestFixtures 2021-03-18T17:18:42+05:30 logger.go:66: Destroy complete!
Resources: 1 destroyed.
--- PASS: TestFixtures (96.62s)
PASS
ok      basictests      96.913s
```

It is possible to write two tests, with each having its own assert statement. For example, one of the tests could be named TestResourceGroupName and the other TestResourceGroupIdentifier. The result of the execution test is shown next. I have condensed the output for brevity.

```
=== RUN   TestResourceGroupName
TestResourceGroupName 2021-03-25T19:37:04+05:30 logger.go:66: Destroy
complete! Resources: 1 destroyed.
--- PASS: TestResourceGroupName (87.09s)

=== RUN   TestResourceGroupIdentifier
TestResourceGroupIdentifier 2021-03-25T19:38:30+05:30 logger.go:66: Destroy
complete! Resources: 1 destroyed.
--- PASS: TestResourceGroupIdentifier (85.97s)
PASS
ok      firsttest       173.542s
```

It is not a good practice to separate tests in this way. When there is a multiple test function, each function goes through the process of Assemble-Act-Assert, and each of them will provision and tear down the resources. It can become a time-consuming process if there are multiple test cases. This example shows the possibilities, but there are better ways to organize the tests.

It is a good practice to write a single high-order function for unit testing each scenario for a single resource. For example, if we want to unit test Azure App services, there should be one Test function to test its diagnostic logging, and other functions for testing virtual network integration, custom domain name, app settings, etc. Within each of these functions, there could be multiple assert statements. The Golang testing framework provides a run function that helps to define subtests with the added advantage of not defining them as separate functions. This will become clear with the help of an example.

The previous code has been refactored to include a run function; however, the test case remains the same, and the code in bold shows the changes compared to the previous test code. Each run is a golang sub-routine and gets executed parallely on separate threads.

```go
func TestResourceGroup(t *testing.T) {
    // Setting resource group configuration, including name and rg_identifier
    // the subscriptionId, clientId, Client_secret and tenantId is not
    //    hard-coded in script. Rather it is read as environmental variable
    resourceGroupName := random.UniqueId()
    subscriptionID := os.Getenv("SUBSCRIPTION_ID")
    clientID := os.Getenv("Client_ID")
    tenantID := os.Getenv("Tenant_ID")
    clientSecret := os.Getenv("Client_Secret")
    resourceGroupId := fmt.Sprintf("/subscriptions/%s/resourceGroups/%s",
    subscriptionID,resourceGroupName)

    // Terraform configuration used for the test. This helps in generating
    //    the Terraform command
    terraformOptions := &terraform.Options{
        // The path to where our Terraform code is located
        TerraformDir: "../fixtures",

        // Variables to pass to our Terraform code using -var options
        Vars: map[string]interface{}{
            "rg_name":   resourceGroupName,
            "location": "west europe",
            "client_id" : clientID,
            "client_secret" : clientSecret,
            "subscription_id" : subscriptionID,
            "tenant_id" : tenantID,
        },
    }

    // This will cleanup all resources provisioned as part of test as final step
    defer terraform.Destroy(t, terraformOptions)
```

```
// This will init and plan the resources and fail the test if there are
    any errors
terraform.InitAndPlan(t, terraformOptions)

// This will apply the resources and fail the test if there are any errors
terraform.Apply(t, terraformOptions)

t.Run("ResourceGroupNameCheck", func(t * testing.T) {
        // This will pull output values generated as part of Terraform
        script execution
        rg_identifier := terraform.Output(t, terraformOptions,
        "rg_identifier")

        // Comparing the actual and expected values. Fail is they do
        not match
        assert.Equal(t, resourceGroupName, rg_identifier)

})

t.Run("ResourceGroupIdentifierCheck", func(t * testing.T) {
    // This will pull output values generated as part of Terraform
    script execution
    rg_id := terraform.Output(t, terraformOptions, "rg_id")

    // Comparing the actual and expected values. Fail is they do not match
    assert.Equal(t, resourceGroupId, rg_id)
})

}

TestResourceGroup 2021-03-25T20:11:34+05:30 logger.go:66: Destroy complete!
Resources: 1 destroyed.
--- PASS: TestResourceGroup (76.25s)
    --- PASS: TestResourceGroup/ResourceGroupNameCheck (0.64s)
    --- PASS: TestResourceGroup/ResourceGroupIdentifierCheck (0.60s)
=== RUN   TestResourceGroupIdentifier
```

Parallel Execution

Golang is highly configurable with regard to the parallel execution of the tests. There are default settings for parallel execution, and they can be overridden. Terratest makes use of Golang's parallel features for parallel test execution.

There are multiple levels of parallel execution in Golang.

- *Across packages*: Tests can be defined within different packages, and that impacts the level of parallel unit test execution.

- *Within a package*: Within a package, there can be multiple test functions and goroutines, and they also potentially execute in parallel.

The unit tests can be distributed across packages, and they can run in parallel using the -p option available with the go test command. For example, if we have three packages and we want to execute tests in them in parallel across packages, the command shown next can be used:

go test -p 3

The functions within a package will run sequentially by default, and they can be configured to execute in parallel using the parallel function available with the testing package. There are two steps to be undertaken for running tests in parallel within a package.

- Adding the t.Parallel() function call within test functions
- Configuring the -parallel option while executing the tests

The first step requires adding the t.Parallel() function call as the first line of code within the function. A call to the parallel function is a signal that the current function can execute in parallel. Similarly, other functions can also use this function to provide their intent. All such functions with parallel function invocation as the first line will execute in parallel.

The second step is to use the -parallel option along with the go test command. It allows parallel execution of test functions that call t.Parallel. The default value for this option is set to the GOMAXPROCS environment variable. GOMAXPROCS refers to the maximum number of processors/CPU that can be used for executing the threads. By default, it is equal to the number of processors in the system. To view Golang-specific environment variables, the command go env can be executed.

In brief, if we want to run tests in three packages in parallel, along with eight test functions within these packages, the command shown next can be used. This is obviously dependent on the fact that there are eight CPUs available in the system.

```
go test -p 3 -parallel 8
```

Integration Tests

Integration tests, as the name suggests, refer to testing processes and evaluating outcomes after integrating two or more components or resources. While unit tests focus on a single resource when testing IaC, integration tests focus on the integration of multiple resources and validating if they integrate/interact as expected.

Writing integration tests is no different than writing unit tests. It involves the same process of Assemble-Act-Assertion, but with the addition that the output of the first resources might be used as input to the next set of resources and continue down the hierarchy. The next set of resources undergoes the same process of Assemble-Act-Assertion.

This section will use Terraform modules to illustrate the process and steps involved in integration tests. For more information about Terraform modules, refer to Chapter 5.

The structure of the project containing Terraform files with modules is shown next.

IaC is the topmost folder containing a Terraform script for all environments like development, stage, and production. There is a modules folder that contains Terraform modules. The modules are based on single or multiple logically related resources. For example, SQL Server modules will contain resources like SQL Server, SQL Database, firewall, etc., together as a unit. The environments will use resource modules directly to provision resources.

The entire code listing for this project is available with the code repository of this book. See Figure 8-1.

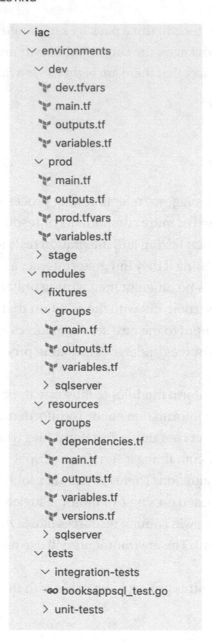

Figure 8-1. *Complete Terraform folder structure including modules and tests*

Integration tests generally include and combine multiple resources or modules. If the tests want to test multiple modules together, they would invoke the fixtures for each module in various combinations. For example, there could be an integration test that will combine resource groups and SQL Server modules to check if they both are compatible and are able to work together. The fixture code for resource group module is shown next:

```
terraform {
  required_providers {
    azurerm = {
      source  = "hashicorp/azurerm"
      version = "=2.51.0"
    }
  }
}

provider "azurerm" {
    features {}
}

module "resource_group" {
    source = "../../resources/groups"
    resourceGroupName = var.resourceGroupName
    resourceGroupLocation = var.resourceGroupLocation
    resourceGroupTags = var.resourceGroupTags
}
```

The fixture code for the SQL Server module is shown next:

```
terraform {
  required_providers {
    azurerm = {
      source  = "hashicorp/azurerm"
      version = "=2.51.0"
    }
  }
}

provider "azurerm" {
    features {}
}

module "sql_server" {
```

```
    source = "../../resources/sqlserver"
    location = var.location
    whitelist_ip_addresses = var.whitelist_ip_addresses
    sql_server_name = var.sql_server_name
    admin_username = var.admin_username
    admin_password = var.admin_password
    database_name = var.database_name
    sql_tags = var.sql_tags
    resource_group_name = var.resourceGroupName
}
```

The resources provisioned by the SQL Server module should in the resource group represented by the resource_group module. There is a direct integration of resources in this case.

The integration test script for this module is shown next. The code listing is similar to the previous script we authored when discussing unit testing. However, since we are doing integration testing, the code consists of two Terraform options structs: one for the resource group module and another for the SQL Server module. The SQL Server module is dependent on the resource group module as it needs to host itself within the resource group. Both the modules are deployed one after another in sequence by using the appropriate parameters and outputs captured. The output from the first module is also passed as the input to the next module. Finally, comparisons are made on the outputs from both the modules on the actual and expected values.

```
// Setting resource group configuration, including name and
    rg_identifier
// the subscriptionId, clientId, Client_secret and tenantId is not
    hard-coded in script. Rather it is read as environmental variable
resourceGroupName := random.UniqueId()
subscriptionID := os.Getenv("SUBSCRIPTION_ID")
resourceGroupId := fmt.Sprintf("/subscriptions/%s/resourceGroups/%s",
subscriptionID,resourceGroupName)
terraformOptions := &terraform.Options{
    TerraformDir: "../../fixtures/groups",

    // Variables to pass to our Terraform code using -var options
    Vars: map[string]interface{}{
```

```
            "resourceGroupName":       resourceGroupName,
            "resourceGroupLocation": "west europe",
            "resourceGroupTags": map[string]string{
                "owner":       "ritesh",
                "environment": "development",
            },
        },
    }

    defer terraform.Destroy(t, terraformOptions)

    terraform.InitAndApply(t, terraformOptions)

    rgname := terraform.Output(t, terraformOptions, "resourceGroupName")
    rgIdentifier := terraform.Output(t, terraformOptions,
    "resourceGroupIdentifier")

    assert.Equal(t, resourceGroupName, rgname)
    assert.Equal(t, resourceGroupId, rgIdentifier)

    sql_server_name := strings.ToLower( fmt.Sprintf("%s%s", random.
    UniqueId(),random.UniqueId()))
    sqlid := fmt.Sprintf("/subscriptions/%s/resourceGroups/%s/providers/Microsoft.
    Sql/servers/%s", subscriptionID, resourceGroupName, sql_server_name)

    sqlfqdn := fmt.Sprintf("%s.database.windows.net", sql_server_name)

    admin_name := fmt.Sprintf("%s%s", random.UniqueId(),random.UniqueId())
    password := fmt.Sprintf("%s%s", random.UniqueId(),random.UniqueId())
    database_name := random.UniqueId()

    terraformOptions1 := &terraform.Options{

        TerraformDir: "../../fixtures/sqlserver",

        Vars: map[string]interface{}{
            "whitelist_ip_addresses":       []string{"0.0.0.0/32"},
            "sql_server_name":    sql_server_name,
            "admin_username":    admin_name,
            "admin_password": password,
            "database_name":       database_name,
```

```
        "resourceGroupName":            rgname,
        "location":                     "west europe",
        "sql_tags": map[string]string{
            "owner":          "ritesh",
            "environment": "development",
        },
    },
}

// This will cleanup all resources provisioned as part of test as final step
defer terraform.Destroy(t, terraformOptions1)

// This will init and plan the resources and fail the test if there are
   any errors
terraform.InitAndPlan(t, terraformOptions1)

// This will apply the resources and fail the test if there are any errors
terraform.Apply(t, terraformOptions1)

// This will pull output values generated as part of Terraform script execution
sql_server_id := terraform.OutputRequired(t, terraformOptions1, "sql_
server_id")
sql_server_fqdn := terraform.Output(t, terraformOptions1, "sql_server_fqdn")
sql_databases_id := terraform.Output(t, terraformOptions1,
"sql_databases_id")

// Comparing the actual and expected values. Fail is they do not match
assert.Equal(t, sqlid, sql_server_id)
assert.Equal(t, sqlfqdn, sql_server_fqdn)

assert.NotEmpty(t, sql_databases_id)
assert.Regexp(t, database_name, sql_databases_id)
```

The integration tests are executed just like unit tests using the Go test command. To execute the integration tests shown earlier in this chapter, ensure there is a folder named integration-tests within the modules folder. It has a single Go test file named booksappsql_test.go. This file contains the integration tests specific to modules developed in Chapter 5. Also, you should refer to the source code accompanying this book to understand each code file.

The `integration-test` folder should be converted into a Go module by executing the following command:

```
go mod init integrationtests
```

This will generate the `.mod` and `.sum` files for all the packages used in the test script. The next command will download the packages used in the current module to the local folder:

```
go mod vendor
```

Once the packages are downloaded, from the same terminal, export the environment variables related to authenticating with Azure using the service principal. You can do this using the commands shown here:

```
export ARM_CLIENT_ID="xxxxxxxx-xxxx-xxxx-xxxxxxxxxxxx"
export ARM_CLIENT_SECRET="xxxxxxxx-xxxx-xxxx-xxxxxxxxxxxx "
export ARM_SUBSCRIPTION_ID="xxxxxxxx-xxxx-xxxx-xxxxxxxxxxxx "
export ARM_TENANT_ID="xxxxxxxx-xxxx-xxxx-xxxxxxxxxxxx "
```

Now, the Terraform modules and fixtures executed as part of the Terratest integration tests can be authenticated to Azure. Finally, from within the context of the `integrationtests` folder, the tests can be executed using the following command:

```
SUBSCRIPTION_ID=9755ffce-e94b-4332-9be8-1ade15e78909 go test -v
```

Here the `SUBSCRIPTION _ID` value is passed explicitly as another environment variable such that the Terratest script can construct a resource group identifier in code to compare the expected and actual values.

The results of the integration test are shown next. Similar multiple integration tests should be written to cover all the modules and resources in various combinations that are applicable for the application or solution.

```
TestResourceGroupAndSQLServer 2021-07-04T17:26:33+05:30 logger.go:66: module.resource_group.azurerm_resource_group.
TestResourceGroupAndSQLServer 2021-07-04T17:26:33+05:30 logger.go:66:
TestResourceGroupAndSQLServer 2021-07-04T17:26:33+05:30 logger.go:66: Destroy complete! Resources: 1 destroyed.
TestResourceGroupAndSQLServer 2021-07-04T17:26:33+05:30 logger.go:66:
--- PASS: TestResourceGroupAndSQLServer (325.19s)
PASS
ok      integrationtests        325.664s
```

Summary

Unit and integration testing has become an integral part of both Terraform and IaC. To ensure that Terraform scripts are authored and executed such that they produce expected outcomes to both provision and manage resources has become an important factor for the adoption of IaC. Terratest is the leading framework for testing Terraform scripts. It is written in Golang and uses Golang's test infrastructure to author and execute both unit and integration tests. Terratest provides packages that help to capture different types of outputs from the Terraform output command, to utilize packages for different types of assertions between expected and actual values, and to utilize different functions to execute Terraform commands after a comprehensive configuration.

This chapter covered all the major concepts related to Terratest and testing, including unit testing and integration testing with regard to IaC. It showed ways to capture map and list outputs apart from primitive string and other data types.

Now that you've finished this chapter, you should be comfortable writing your own unit and integration tests for Terraform scripts. The next chapter will focus on best practices related to implementing Terraform configurations and its components.

CHAPTER 9

Terraform Best Practices

Finally, we are at the last chapter of this book. Terraform offers multiple ways to implement configurations. Technically, they are all valid solutions, and Terraform will not complain about which one you use. However, it is important to evaluate whether the chosen technique is generic, reusable, extensible, secure, and promotes collaboration. This chapter is about implementing Terraform configurations using best practices. This chapter will cover the important practices to remember while using Terraform features like providers, variables, versioning, authentication to name a few.

General

It is a good practice to create reusable modules and consume them when provisioning resources using Terraform configurations. This will ensure standardization of resources and also ensure resources are provisioned in a consistent way.

A naming convention should be established based on organizational policies and standards. There should be a naming convention for Terraform resources, variables, and outputs. Generally, lowercase letters and underscore separators are used when naming Terraform resources and artifacts.

It is not a good practice to hard-code strings and configuration values. There could be places where hard-coding is acceptable depending on the requirements and the project; however, it is generally best avoided. Use local, output, and input variables to make the configurations generic and reusable.

Terraform does not expect the entire configuration to be in a single file. The Terraform configurations can be broken into multiple physical files each containing certain logical parts of the configuration. All these files within a folder are assembled

© Ritesh Modi 2021
R. Modi, *Deep-Dive Terraform on Azure*, https://doi.org/10.1007/978-1-4842-7328-9_9

together by Terraform during execution. It is a good practice to break down the files as suggested here:

- Main.tf - should only contain the Terraform modules declaration and associated configuration.

- Variables.tf - should contain all variable definitions.

- Locals.tf - should contain all local variable definitions and expressions

- Outputs.tf - should contain all output variables.

- Providers.tf - should contain provider configuration and versioning information.

Input Variables

Input variables should be declared with data types that best define the value constraints.

Input variables should use sensitive attribute if it will be hold any sensitive data. This will not display the values on the console.

All input variables should have a `description` attribute with the appropriate literal value assigned.

Input variables should also validate the incoming values using validation rules. An example is shown here:

```
variable "storage_name" {
  type        = string
  description = "The name of Azure storage account."

  validation {
    condition     = length(var.storage_name) < 3 && length(var.storage_name
                    ) >  24
    error_message = "The storage name should be between 3 and 24 characters."
  }
}
```

Finally, it is a good practice to avoid providing a default value to input variables. A default value is appropriate for variables in cases where the value does not determine the flow of execution.

Output Variables

Output variables should return values that are sensitive in nature. Output variables can use optional "sensitive" attribute to denote the output value as sensitive. It accepts true/false as value.

All output variables should have the `description` attribute with the appropriate text assigned to it.

Local Variables

Use local variables when the value is not user-dependent or user-supplied. The value is used multiple times within the configuration. It can also be used to sanitize and standardize user-supplied input variables.

Versioning

A well-designed Terraform configuration relies on providers and modules for most of its functionalities. There are two distinct versions that Terraform developers should be aware of.

- The Terraform version is the version of the Terraform binary. It is a good practice to provide the upper and lower versions for the Terraform binary dependency to ensure that the configuration does not break due to version incompatibilities. Specify the Terraform version in the root module within the `terraform` section, as shown here:

```
terraform {
  required_version = "~> 0.14"
}
```

It is a good practice to limit the lower as well as upper version for the Terraform binary. The ~> operator sets both the upper and lower constraints. For example, ~> 0.14 means that the lower boundary for the version is 0.14.0, and the upper boundary is the version less than 0.15.0.

- Each Terraform module also has a version associated with it. There are root modules and child modules. Root modules are the main way the Terraform configurations are applied. They are the entry point within the Terraform configuration—the topmost configuration. The child modules are the modules used and invoked by the root module directly or indirectly by other child modules. The root module, just like the Terraform binary, should limit the upper and lower version constraints; however, the child modules should definitely have a lower-version constraint and optionally can have an upper-version constraint.

Provider

Providers provides the resource definition needed by Terraform configuration. These providers have their own development lifecycle and release versions. It is important to have a dependency on specific version of the provider as shown next.

```
terraform {
  required_providers {
    azurerm = {
      source  = "hashicorp/azurerm"
      version = "~> 2.54.0"
    }
  }

  required_version = "~> 0.14"
}
```

The `required_providers` variable defines the local name `"azurerm"` along with the path and version values for the provider. This sets up the lower and upper version constraints for the provider.

If multiple providers from same source are used, it is prudent to provide different local names for them. Using the local names' subsequent provider configuration can be provided.

The provider configuration should be used to configure the provider, as shown here:

```
provider "azurerm" {
  client_id        = var.client_id
  client_secret    = var.client_secret
  subscription_id = var.subscription_id
  tenant_id        = var.tenant_id
  features {
    key_vault {
      purge_soft_delete_on_destroy      = false
      recover_soft_deleted_key_vaults = false
    }
  }
}
```

The provider configuration generally consists of authentication related attributes alongside other attributes that helps in configuring the behavior of the provider.

Provisioners

Avoid executing local or remote files from Terraform. They can have unexpected results and can render the configuration indeterministic. This is primarily because the script content can change without Terraform having any knowledge about it.

Provisioners allow execution of scripts locally as well as remotely. The execution of scripts brings in additional capabilities that are generally not pragmatic in configuration based languages. Executing scripts can pose security challenges. Since the script is external to the configuration, it is possible that the script has undergone changes and is compromised.

If any provisioners are used in configuration, the file content should be verified before being used. This can easily be done by capturing the hash of the file and comparing it before executing the file from Terraform.

Provisioners are generally tied to an existing resource within the configuration that has the capability to execute a script like a virtual machine on Azure. Use the "null_ resource" resource if the script should be executed without it being associated with any specific resource. The null_resource resource is available from the null plugin.

It is also good to explicitly mention whether the script should continue to execute when there is an error or stop its execution.

Lifecycle

Terraform compares the properties of each resource to determine whether it should update the resource. While some of the properties can be updated in place, there are properties that demand a resource be deleted and then re-created.

For each resource declared within the Terraform configuration, it is prudent to mention when the resource should be updated. There are properties that might not be significant enough to bring about updates to a resource. The `lifecycle` section provides `ignore_changes` attributes that accept a list of resource properties. Any changes to them will not update the resource.

The `lifecycle` section also provides the `prevent_destroy` attribute and as a good practice should be used for resources in a production environment. This attribute set to `true` ensures that the resource will not be destroyed, and Terraform will raise an error when it is used to destroy the environment.

Testing

Each module, environment configuration, and resource should have a separate unit test file. For example, Azure storage account unit tests should be separate from a resource group unit tests and they can be better managed if they happen to be in different files.

Each test case should be implemented either as a separate function or as a subtest within a parent function. This helps in multiple ways. The test command outputs each subtest and function separately, and this helps in easily identifying tests that are passing versus those that are failing. It results in better maintainability of the implemented tests.

Each test should be executed in parallel to other tests within the package and across multiple test packages.

The retry mechanism provided by the `TerraformOptions` struct should be used with a retry policy to ensure that the test results are eventually the least impacted because of the nonavailability of an infrastructure resource like network connectivity.

Go tests by default are configured to execute for 10 minutes. They time out in the case of a longer execution. It is a good practice to add a timeout option with the value 0 for an infinite time or a value that is more suitable for the tests.

State Management

Terraform state should be stored remotely. The remote state should be protected and allow only authorized access. It should be accessible using the TLS latest version and should have a means for authentication and authorization before accessing the state file. Finally, the remote state should be encrypted both at rest and in transit.

Module

The main purposes of modules are reusability, standardization, and enforcing organizational compliance related requirements. Modules should parameterize all aspects that could change between environments and projects. They should not have any hard-coded values for attributes unless it is known that they will not evolve or change in the future.

Modules should declare local variables for internal variables and parameter transformations. For example, local variables can be used to lowercase parameters for storage account names.

Modules should output all the resource configurations provisioned by them. This will ensure that different teams can use any of the exposed values either for passing the values to another resource as a parameter or for unit testing purposes.

A module might not contain just a single resource. It can contain multiple resources that have the same lifecycle (deploy, manage, and teardown) and should logically be together. For example, both the Azure App Service Plan and Azure App Service can be declared in the same module.

Workspaces

Workspaces are part of a Terraform back-end construct. Each Terraform configuration is associated with a back end, and by default a "default" workspace is used to store a state file. Multiple workspaces can be defined for the same configuration, and each workspace will have a unique state file. For development and test purposes, instead of copying the configuration files and generating a new state file, it is preferred to create a new workspace and execute all the development and testing processes. Once you're confident of the changes, the workspace can be switched back to the default workspace. The default workspace should be related to the production state file and other back-end configuration.

It is not advised to use workspaces to create different environments such as development, testing, and production. Create new environments using different configuration values and separate the back end, including the state files.

Terraform provides a `count` and `foreach` mechanism to generate multiple dynamic resources in a loop. It is generally preferred to use `foreach` rather than `count` to generate dynamic resources. The reason behind this is that `count` produces an array of resources, while `foreach` produces a map of resources. It is much easier and less error prone to work with maps compared to arrays while deleting and updating individual resources generated as part of the dynamic resources.

Authentication

Terraform scripts should authenticate with Azure before they can provision and manage resources. Terraform provides multiple ways to authenticate to Azure. Using service principals and managed identities are preferred mechanisms to authenticate to Azure. For authentication to Azure, service principal information should not be hard-coded within the scripts. This sensitive information should be supplied either using:

–   Terraform variables or

–   Environment variables

Terraform provides predefined environment variables for authentication-related sensitive information, and these variables should be used for configuring authentication.

Another best practice for Azure authentication is to use the Azure CLI authentication along with Service Principal.

CI/CD Pipeline

Terraform files should be stored in a repository and version controlled. Multiple developers should be able to work on the same scripts in parallel and collaborate on them.

Storing files in a version control system also helps in reverting to a good well-known version.

The Terraform continuous integration process should start when a pull request is accepted using a build verification pipeline. The build verification pipeline is the build pipeline that was discussed in chapter related to CI/CD pipelines. The Build process should execute if any changes are made to Terraform-related files.

No secrets should be stored within the version control repositories and in pipelines. Azure DevOps provides a facility to use service principals with service connections. These service connections and service principals can be configured by an administrator to establish connectivity to Azure, and pipeline developers can use the service connection in their pipelines.

The pipeline developers should fetch the necessary secrets from Azure Key Vault using the service connection. This can be done using the `AzureKeyVault` task provided by Azure DevOps. These secrets should at minimal relate to accessing Terraform remote state and connectivity to Azure.

Summary

This is the last chapter of this book. A lot has been covered in this book with regard to working with the Azure cloud with Terraform. Each chapter covered the details of a prominent feature of Terraform. In this chapter, the best practices related to all those concepts, features, and Terraform architecture were brought together to provide you with some of the practices you should adopt while working with Terraform in general and also alongside Azure. The Terraform best practices related to variables, outputs, providers, versioning, modules, state management, CI/CD pipelines, and security.

Index

U

Printed in the United States
by Baker & Taylor Publisher Services